SHAPING ETERNITY

An Invitation onto the Road Less Traveled

BY
JOHN ZABUKOVEC

WORD & SPIRIT
PUBLISHING

Unless otherwise indicated, Scripture quotations are taken from the New King James Version®. Copyright © 1982 by Thomas Nelson. Used by permission. All rights reserved.

Scripture quotations marked NLT are taken from the Holy Bible, New Living Translation, copyright © 1996, 2004, 2015 by Tyndale House Foundation. Used by permission of Tyndale House Publishers, Inc., Carol Stream, Illinois 60188. All rights reserved.

Shaping Eternity
An Invitation onto the Road Less Traveled
Copyright 2024 by John Zabukovec
ISBN: 978-1-685730-60-4

Published by Word and Spirit Publishing
P.O. Box 701403
Tulsa, Oklahoma 74170
wordandspiritpublishing.com

Printed in the United States of America. All rights reserved under International Copyright Law. Content and/or cover may not be reproduced in whole or in part in any form without the expressed written consent of the Publisher.

CONTENTS

Foreword v

Introduction vii

1 The Beginning 1

2 Our Identities in Christ...11

3 The Great Commission..17

4 The Gospel...25

5 Rivers of Living Water...33

6 The Gifts of the Holy Spirit...39

7 Healing..49

8 Hearing from God...57

9 Divine Appointments..67

10 Waiting on God...77

11 Rejection 83

12 Overcoming Apathy..91

13 No Time..99

14 Not Knowing What to Say..105

15 God's Fingerprints 113

16 Divine Protection..121

17 Love 127

Conclusion 135

Foreword

I FIRST met John Zabukovec years ago, when he began participating in our summer Mission Tours in the Philippines. From then until now, I have consistently been impressed with his love for God, and his dedication to keep the commandments of the Lord – starting with the Great Commission of Mark 16:15-18. Truly, John is an end-times example of what every believer's life should be about – which is making oneself available to the Holy Spirit whenever lost and hungry souls are encountered.

John has shared with me the details of many of his on-the-street encounters with people, and I am always so blessed by what the Lord uses him to do and say. Let the contents of this book be your clarion call to get in the game and do something significant for Jesus.

        Apostle Mike Keyes Sr.
        Founder & President: Mike Keyes Ministries International

Introduction

AS FOLLOWERS of Jesus Christ, we have been invited to participate in a great adventure, one in which the path chosen determines our eternity and the eternity of those around us. God's desire is that all would go to heaven and avoid the horror of hell. We each carry within us gifts, talents, and an anointing to help those around us with their burdens. Through Jesus Christ, men and women can be set free; their lives can be changed, and their futures reclaimed. Marriages can be healed, addictions broken, the demon-possessed liberated. Through Christ, depression and anxiety can be shattered, hope restored, the sick made whole, and destinies realized!

There is no map to follow, but there is a guidebook, the Bible; my hope is to inspire others to join the adventure. Throughout this book, I will share encounters I have personally experienced. My walk with God is an ongoing beautiful experience. My growth in relationship with God has been developed by attending great churches and conferences, listening to countless thought-provoking messages, and reading many informative books. Through that process, I have learned so much about God, His Word, and what we are called to do as followers of Jesus.

I have seen the truth of Scripture play out both in spectacular and seemingly ordinary ways. The same Jesus who was healing people more than two thousand years ago is healing lives in my city today. The greatest moves of God within lives that I have seen have not just taken place within the four walls of a building, but in the daily spontaneous and unscripted parts of life amidst the gritty and unkempt parts of the city, where the addicted, the lost, and the mentally ill walk out their lives. I have also seen His presence move at the beaches and the mountains; in stores, planes, Ubers, Lyfts, hotels, and gyms.

The same Holy Spirit who was drawing men into a relationship with Jesus in the book of Acts is currently operating on street corners, in parks, in individual conversations and group settings. To the person passing by, it would likely not even warrant a second look. To the individual with whom the appointment has been orchestrated, however, it is life-changing and takes many forms. An encounter of God's love reminds them that they are not forgotten, may bring them healing from an incurable disease, or the greatest miracle of all, could lead them to accept Jesus as their Lord and Savior, ensuring their eternity in heaven.

When I go out to share the love of Jesus, I have no idea what to expect other than it will likely include a mix of rejection, indifference, and those who are receptive. The interaction I have with those I meet may be sensational or seemingly unremarkable.

There was a season in my life when I was drawn to the gifts of the Holy Spirit. These gifts were displayed by Jesus in the Gospels with healing the sick, operating in the prophetic, giving words of knowledge, and performing unusual miracles. In John 14:12, Jesus gives believers the assurance of what our ministry will look like when we follow Him: ". . . and greater works than these will he do." The disciples and the apostle Paul show us by their example found in Scripture that what Jesus said was true. The truth of the promises Jesus gave us are also demonstrated through the miraculous stories I have heard about the generals in the faith, including

Introduction

Aimee Semple McPherson, Reinhard Bonnke, William Seymour, Bayless Conley, and Mike Keyes. While I wanted to see miracles happen in my own life, it wasn't until I took what I learned, began to take risks, and made myself available to the Lord in my everyday life that I saw remarkable moves of God. The miraculous moves of God that I desired to see began to take place as I stepped out in faith and offered to pray for people in my day-to-day life. The more frequently I prayed for people, the more frequently I saw the Holy Spirit move. God would reveal Himself in new and exciting ways through my *increased availability*. While I wanted to see God move, it wasn't until I listened and obeyed that I began to see the supernatural touching those around me on a regular basis.

My story has been rich and prepared by God. I have had thousands of individual encounters, with God's presence impacting lives. The encounters I have with people are simple. They are also often awkward because praying for a stranger is not common. At times, I sense in my heart instructions from God about people or situations. As I act on the insights God gives me, I see how deeply they impact the people I talk to. Most of the encounters I have with people do not come with any insights other than I know that God loves the people I am talking to, and He wants to help them. Just because you don't hear something from God, doesn't mean you don't act. In these situations, I offer to pray for people in faith trusting that God will express His radical love for them in a very personal way. I trust that God will guide the conversation, and He does. The people I pray with often share how amazed they are by the power of prayer and how it encourages them in the trial they are facing. Many people will share how they were feeling alone or forgotten before we talked. Through prayer and the conversation we have, God reminds them how much He loves them and is actively working on their behalf. For everything I have observed God do in each encounter, I am convinced that He is accomplishing exponentially more than I can perceive and only in eternity will we fully understand the fruit that comes from our obedience in fulfilling the Great Commission.

I do not believe you are reading this book by accident. Our time together is not a coincidence. I believe it has been ordained, orchestrated by God. Perhaps you are like me and desire to see greater moves of God in your life. Perhaps you are new to the faith and are still learning what is possible through your relationship with Jesus. Perhaps you are seeing God operate in your life and the lives of others, but you want to see more of Him. Wherever you find yourself, my prayer is that the Holy Spirit will draw you deeper into the place of risk and further along on the road less traveled. Since we are all originals created by God, it is unlikely that our walks will look the same. You travel in different circles, have different routines, and know different people. The common space we share is that God has prepared good works for each of us to walk in, that risk in faith will be required , and that being obedient to the voice of God will be foundational. If you are at all like me, God has been tugging at your heart to walk closer with Him and step into the next season of what you are called to do. The purpose of this book is to inspire and encourage you in your adventure with God. I want to help you walk in the fullness of all you have been called to do—what Jesus died on the cross to accomplish in order to equip you in that beautiful calling. My hope is that we will be able to talk someday and share stories of all that we saw God do through our obedience and simple availability.

1

The Beginning

HOW DID this all start anyway? Have I always been bold in praying for others and sharing my faith? The answer is that boldness and zeal for Jesus is not something I was born with. For much of my life and the initial years I walked with God, I had very little confidence in spiritual matters. I figured I would have to have specialized training to be a priest or pastor. As I learned more about the life of Jesus, the disciples, the life of Paul, and the modern generals in the faith, I developed a hunger to see more of the miraculous. In fact, I was intimidated and did not feel particularly gifted for what God asked me to do.

My first experience preaching the Gospel was not by my design. In fact, when the call came, my first response was to respond like Jonah did when God called him to preach to the Ninevites. While I did not stow away on a ship or get swallowed by a large fish, I was just as obstinate.

The year was 2010, and there had been a massive earthquake in Haiti. The island was in total shambles, and the UN was there to help keep the peace. In faith, I volunteered to go on a mission trip to help build a medical clinic in Port-au-Prince. One morning, our ministry host informed us we were going to minister in a local prison that day. He asked the group, "Who is going to be preaching today?" He was met with awkward silence from the group. When I heard the question, my initial thought was, *Definitely not me!* When he did not get a response, the man asked again—and was met with the same awkward silence. Not to be deterred, he asked a third time, and finally a member of the team volunteered to share a little. While this process went on, I just knew I was supposed to volunteer. God was drawing me into something so beautiful and powerful, but it was entirely outside of my comfort zone. In my heart, I told God that if He wanted me to share my heart at the prison that day, He should have the man ask the question again, and I would do it.

I was so spiritual I didn't even have my Bible with me! When the van pulled out of the compound, I asked one of the other team members if I could borrow their Bible. God put the story of Joseph on my heart, so I began to prepare a message based on his life. The prison was not far in distance, but the roads were very bad so our travel was extremely slow. The whole way there, my mind was bombarded by thoughts of the large penitentiaries that are depicted in movies: multiple stories high, filled with rowdy prisoners who were yelling, lighting toilet paper on fire, banging cups on prison doors, etc. As the thoughts came, I just put them out of my mind and kept working on my message.

When the van pulled up to the prison, the man once again asked who would preach, and I told him I would. As it turned out, this was not a large prison but something that resembled a strip mall with loads of people, stores, and a section that was, in fact, a prison. There I was facing two very large cells that were maybe 12 feet by 12 feet in size, and they were both filled with men. Much to my surprise, there was a man in one of the cells from Orange County, California.

Because I don't speak Haitian Creole, I had an interpreter, and we were both given bullhorns. As we prepared to start, people from the street

The Beginning

started to crowd into the open area to see what was going on. I shared a message from the life of Joseph as the interpreter translated for me. The message I shared was about how God never wastes a trial and that He was preparing Joseph for a big job through his challenges. God took Joseph from the bottom to become the second-most-powerful man in Egypt—all in a single day. Regardless of where we are in life, God has a great plan for our lives. I concluded the message, gave an invitation to accept Christ and instructed the people that if they would like to accept Jesus as their Savior, they should raise their hands. In both cells, hands from the men shot up. *Much to my surprise*, a man and woman also stepped out of the crowd on the street to accept Christ. I was stunned that the people who came to see what we were doing at the prison were impacted by the Gospel. All glory to God!

This experience taught me that God is faithful and ignited a spark in my heart that God fanned into a flame. That flame has grown to be a fire and a zeal for seeing the lost saved that continues to burn in me to this day. Over the years, God has expanded my heart and comfort zone from the construction projects I did for Him initially to actual evangelism. A big turning point in this journey was when I went on a mission trip with Mike Keyes Ministries International in 2015. At a volunteer fair one weekend at Cottonwood Church, I heard about this ministry and the amazing crusades they held in the Philippines. The person shared how it was like being in the book of Acts, with miraculous healing and all of the decisions they saw being made for Jesus. That was all I needed to hear, so I signed up to be a part of one later that year.

The trip was all that I hoped for and more. We traveled in the mountains to different villages and schools. The team went door-to-door inviting people who needed healing to come to the meeting for prayer. Later in the day, we would conduct a service in the center of the village, where we would do praise and worship, share the Gospel, and pray for the sick. The Holy Spirit moved mightily in response to the Gospel being shared, with many people making decisions for Christ in every service. God moved in beautiful and powerful ways healing the sick. At the end of the service, anyone who was healed could come up and give a testimony about how God had healed them. God healed people of headaches, nausea, and goiters—one man even had the bones in his arm realign—and many other conditions were cured in response to prayer. After six days of ministry, God had changed my heart for missions, and my passion for evangelism only grew.

The following year, I returned to the Philippines with both of my sons to work with MKMI to pray for the sick and reach the lost. Early one morning, I was on the fourth floor of the compound doing my morning devotions when God spoke to my heart about what was next for me. The encounter was simple and powerful, as God put Ezekiel 3:11 on my heart:

> *"And go, get to the captives, to the children of your people, and speak to them and tell them, 'Thus says the Lord God,' whether they hear, or whether they refuse."*
>
> —Ezekiel 3:11

As I read this Scripture, the *logos* became *rhema* and spoke directly to my heart. I knew exactly what God wanted me to do—and it scared me. God wanted me to take what I was doing in the Philippines and take it home to my own country. Doing ministry in a foreign land has always been easier for me, even though it is often conducted in a language I don't understand and in a culture that is unfamiliar. God was asking me to take the Gospel to my own neighborhood, city and into my day-to-day life. The fear of man is a real obstacle and God was asking me to face this fear head on. While it was scary, it was absolutely something I was willing to do for Him.

The Beginning

When I returned home from that trip, it was time to start what God asked me to do. As a first step, I looked into what I could do locally. Cottonwood Church had an outreach team that would go out twice a month to share the love of Jesus with people on the streets of Long Beach and Huntington Beach, California. This was the team I began to work with to *break my fear and expand my capacity for risk-taking*. Street evangelism in the bar scene comes with a healthy dose of rejection. There was a time in my life when you would never have been able to convince me that I would consider this type of ministry or that it would grow to be my passion. God has brought me to a place of deep desire to walk through the unsavory aspects of rejection to fulfill the Great Commission.

The team would meet on the second and fourth Saturdays of each month at alternating locations. We would meet at the church and then take a shuttle to the location. It was very encouraging to carpool together and pray for the outreach as we headed to the location. The evenings would often be marked by continuous rejection in the beginning. The team needed to pray and persist to see God break through. We knew that God was at work even if we couldn't see it. God's Word does not return void, but it accomplishes that which He sends it forth to do (Isaiah 55:11). Each night, we continued to share the love of Jesus with the people on the street. Inevitably, we would connect with those that God wanted us to meet. God connected us with the lost, the searching, the prideful, the addicted, the hopeless, the anxious, and the depressed. In those connections, those precious people would realize they were being pursued by the radical love of the Father: The God of the universe who knows them. The God who knows them so intimately that He literally knows the number of hairs on their heads (Luke 12:7). The God who knows their hopes, their fears, and their radical potential. When someone comes to the realization of who God is and how much He loves them, it is powerful and life-changing for them. Those moments are so holy, so beautiful, and so priceless.

To be a part of them is a profound privilege, something for which I am immensely thankful. *The power of these divine appointments easily dwarfs any disappointment that we could experience as a result of rejection during the evening.*

On one of my early adventures back at home, I went out with the outreach team to Huntington Beach for street evangelism. At first, this made me feel very uncomfortable, but I did it anyway. Once I tried it, I really enjoyed it. God gives you the grace to do what He has called you to do even though it may not feel like it in the moment. There were many who were not interested in what we were sharing, but there was a homeless man who was willing to talk to me.. The man was not walking with God and needed a breakthrough in his life. I was able to pray with him to rededicate his life to Christ and for breakthrough in his life. After the prayer, a cello player who was playing for money approached me to encourage me. He told me that he had listened to the whole conversation and that I was doing a good thing and needed to continue. I was amazed that God would use that man to encourage me after I did what He asked me to do. God has placed people just like that cello player all through my life to encourage me to continue in what He has asked me to do.

That same evening, I noticed three men walking together, and two of them had the tracts we were handing out. I struck up a conversation and offered a tract to the man who didn't have one. As we talked, the men shared that they were Muslim students from Afghanistan. Undeterred, I asked if they needed prayer for anything, and they all wanted prayer for their education. I prayed for them, that God would give them a grace for their studies and reveal to them His amazing plan for their lives. When I concluded the prayer, I asked if they had a relationship with Jesus, and they said they did not. I shared my testimony, the Gospel, and gave those men an invitation to accept Christ. All three prayed with me to accept Jesus as their Savior—all glory to God!

The Beginning

At the end of the evening, the team was debriefing about all that happened during the outreach. I learned that those three men had been approached by others in the group. The first ones to approach them were strongly rejected. Subsequent attempts led to greater receptivity until they got to me. The Holy Spirit had been working on their hearts as they walked down Main Street. This experience stuck with me because it was an example of how God works. One plants, one waters, and it is ultimately God who brings in the harvest at His appointed time. We never know where our interaction with people will land in their salvation journey, but we can be confident that God can be trusted to work it out. We simply need to be obedient in the part we play in His beautiful plan.

The outreach opportunities proved to be both powerful and fulfilling, but we only conducted them twice a month. I began to wonder what would happen if I just did the same things during the course of my normal life and routine. The heart behind it would be the same, but the tactics would change. Since I traveled quite often, I spent a fair amount of time in Ubers, hotels, restaurants, and airports while on my journeys. These locations proved to later be where God expanded my thoughts of what is possible in surprising and powerful ways.

By being available, even on a business trip, I made good use of my Uber time. One of the reasons I like Uber or Lyft so much is you have a defined amount of time to talk to the driver. One approach I have found to be very effective is to let the driver know that I pray for people and see God do amazing things in their lives. I will then share a few testimonies about God answering prayer across a wide variety of areas, including physical sickness; financial challenges; problems with a marriage or kids; anxiety; depression; and difficulties at work. This helps to both build faith and open a door for prayer for that person or their loved ones.

One such example happened years ago: On the way to the airport, I asked my Uber driver if he needed prayer for anything. He requested prayer to stop drinking and for his family. With this door open, I dug deeper . . . it turned out he didn't feel worthy of going to church. He had attended a church by his house, but no one had ever greeted him or made him feel welcome, so he never went back. I shared the Gospel with him, and he accepted Christ. The Holy Spirit moved in a powerful way during that encounter and his countenance totally changed. I always enjoy seeing big, muscular guys with tattoos experience the God of the universe—it is so awesome! He left a different man than the one I'd met when I got in the car. I gave him a copy of the book of John and invited him to Cottonwood Church. All glory to God!

Hotels are also a great place where God moves in powerful and unexpected ways. These encounters happen with both the staff and the guests. God is so remarkable in the profoundly unique ways that He reaches people. We often love our routines and predictability. We find the process that works, and then we rinse and repeat. While God can use this, as He can use anything, my experience with Him is that He regularly flips the script in how He reaches people. This is why it is so important to listen when God puts people on our heart and tells us how He wants us to reach them. This next story is an example.

I was in Sacramento, California having a conversation with the night manager of a hotel. As we talked, I shared that I often pray for people and see God do remarkable things in their lives. The man shared that he had friends who did the same thing, and he accepted prayer for his life. When the prayer concluded, I continued on with my day. The next day, as I was walking through the lobby, the same night manger requested prayer for two final exams he had coming up. I prayed very specifically for his request, that the Holy Spirit would guide him to study the right things and that God would give him grace not only to operate according to his ability but to perform even above his natural ability.

As I walked through the lobby the next day, lost in my thoughts, I heard the night manager call out to me. The man excitedly told me that

The Beginning

my prayer had worked, and he went on to tell me how. The first exam went very well; he was prepared for the material that was on it. The man was very confident that he had aced the test. Next, he explained that when he received the second exam, he reviewed it and saw there were errors in the exam. He brought these to the attention of the professor, who went on to give everyone in the class "freebies" on those particular questions. God had literally answered the specific prayer I had prayed. The man went on to explain how blown away he was, as he was not even religious.

This shows the personality of God and His radical love for us. Even before we acknowledge Him or walk with Him, He is doing beautiful things for us. I shared my testimony, including the Gospel, and I gave this man the invitation to accept Christ. The night manager accepted and received Jesus as his Lord and Savior right there in the lobby of that hotel. God had planned and orchestrated a beautiful salvation journey for that man that night. The adventure we have been invited into is both beautiful and holy.

Since I traveled often, I began to be open to being used by God in airports and during flights. Just like any other location where there are people, in those locations there is often a mix of people who are open and those who are not. One trip comes to mind that involves a series of events from the rental car shuttle and a couple of flights. The encounters flow out of where I am and what God may put on my heart for the folks who may be around. God may give me something very specific for an individual, or it just might be a nudge toward someone standing next to me and I have nothing to go on at all. The next series is an example of both.

When I got on the rental car bus, I offered to pray for the rental car bus driver, who really wanted someone to pray for her husband as he was having major kidney problems. I shared a testimony of a Christian brother I know whom God had healed of kidney failure without an operation and was able to come off dialysis. God encouraged her greatly through the testimony, and she experienced the Holy Spirit when I prayed for her.

While I was later waiting to board the plane, a man in a sea of people stood out to me; the word *awesome* came to mind, as well as the nudge that I should share that word with him. Just as I was about to walk over, I saw a coworker get off a plane whom I had not seen in a long time and we had a brief conversation. When we finished talking, the man had moved away and was then in line to talk to an agent. When I was sitting on the plane later, however, the thought came to me again, so I turned around and saw him twenty rows back, sitting by a window but I did not engage him at that time. In the meantime, I offered to pray for the flight attendant who was serving first class; he was respectful but not interested.

When the plane landed, I waited for the man God had pointed out to disembark, and I then told him what God had put on my heart. He was surprised and really blessed by the encounter. I offered to pray for him, and he shared he was struggling with finances. I suggested we stop walking to pray. I prayed for him and spoke the love and promises of Jesus over him. I asked him if he felt that, and he confirmed he did. I told him that what he experienced was the Holy Spirit. He made the comment that I had gotten it right, that I did, in fact, hear from God. This was another reminder that big, stoic guys with beards appreciate a divine encounter in the airport as much as the person sitting next to us in Sunday service.

The more I opened up different areas of my life to being used by God, the more I have seen that God would use that availability in beautiful ways. God's faithfulness both built up my faith to see Him move and increased my appetite to see Him touch the lives of people around me. This brought about a great curiosity to learn more about His promises, learn from Jesus, and the ways in which He moves that I had not yet experienced but sincerely desired to see. God was giving me the desire to see Him move, and as I was available, He gave me the desire of my heart. What God has done for me, He wants to do in and through you as you are available for Him. He will work through you to establish His Kingdom on earth as it is in heaven.

2

Our Identities in Christ

EVEN THOUGH God could move and sovereignly shape eternity entirely on His own, He chooses to share this incredible honor with us. This is still a very difficult thing for me to get my mind around. The perfect God of the universe would choose to use broken people to accomplish a perfect plan—a plan where heaven and hell hang in the balance for people around us: The people we know and have long relationships with. The people in our lives who are casual acquaintances, and those who are total strangers who could be in the path of our usual routine or onetime errands. This is both a beautiful opportunity and a great responsibility.

When we receive Jesus as our Lord and Savior, we become new creations in Him. Through His sacrifice, we are given something so precious that we could never earn through personal effort or merit. We are adopted into His family. We are given the assurance of heaven as we step into eternity. If this was all there was it would be radical, and more than enough to thank Him for eternity. We serve a God who is amazing and incredibly generous. Not only do we get to spend eternity with Him, but He invites us into an incredible adventure with Him for the balance of our appointed days. Eternity is a very long time. We will all spend eternity somewhere, either in heaven or hell. God's desire is that none would perish, but that all would have eternal life.

> *Therefore, if anyone is in Christ, he is a new creation; old things have passed away; behold, all things have become new. Now all things are of God, who has reconciled us to Himself through Jesus Christ, and has given us the ministry of reconciliation, that is, that God was in Christ reconciling the world to Himself, not imputing their trespasses to them, and has committed to us the word of reconciliation.*
>
> —2 Corinthians 5:17–19

We have been given so much through our relationship with Jesus. We have been born again and are new creations in Jesus. He has given us power and gifts to walk out the calling on our lives. This also comes with a great responsibility, as it says in this Scripture that He has given us the ministry of reconciliation. Jesus paid such a terrible price to see our sins forgiven through His sacrifice on the cross, and yet He turns around and gives the ministry of reconciliation to us. If we are not careful, the weight of this responsibility could be totally crushing if we really understand what it means. Thankfully, we have a Helper in the Holy Spirit, to both will and do what He asks of us.

> *"He who believes in Me, as the Scripture has said, out of his heart will flow rivers of living water."*
>
> —John 7:38

The power of the Holy Spirit is an awesome gift, and the truth of this Scripture is evident when I pray for people and when I share the Gospel. The Holy Spirit operates in a multitude of ways, varying by individual and what each situation needs. The Holy Spirit moves in prayers with believers and those yet to have a relationship with Jesus. The Holy Spirit operates as we share the Gospel, by giving life to what is shared and captivating the listener by the love of the Father. Some describe the moving of the Holy Spirit as a feeling of peace; others experience goose bumps; some describe the Holy Spirit as a strong feeling of love; some people will tear up; others will shed a few tears; and some will weep deeply. Those who have a relationship with Jesus and know how the Holy Spirit moves will know immediately when He is moving. Others do not know, and we have the opportunity to share with them what they are experiencing. The Holy Spirit moving in this way was promised in the book of Acts:

> *"But you shall receive power when the Holy Spirit has come upon you; and you shall be witnesses to Me in Jerusalem, and in all Judea and Samaria, and to the end of the earth."*
>
> —Acts 1:8

God gives us this power not just to admire it, but to be used for His purpose and glory. This equipping helps us to be set free from our cultural dependence on performance. When we pray for people or share the Gospel, it is God who works through our availability. Therefore, He gets all the glory for the work He performs. If the person we are talking to is not ready to accept Christ, we don't need to carry any condemnation or personalize the rejection. God is sufficient, and we can trust Him to use other means and people to reach the folks who may not be ready yet. This helps us tremendously to be available and to trust Him for the ultimate outcome of reaching those in our lives with the Gospel.

Jesus is our Savior and our example. One of the Scriptures I love and that I have seen in operation regularly in life can be found in the gospel of John:

> *"Most assuredly, I say to you, he who believes in Me, the works that I do he will do also; and greater works than these he will do, because I go to My Father. And whatever you ask in My name, that I will do, that the Father may be glorified in the Son."*
>
> —John 14:12–13

Depending on your translation of the Bible, this is written in red, so we know it is a direct promise from Jesus Himself. For us to truly appreciate the magnitude of this promise and what it means for the life we can live, we must consider what Jesus did during His earthly ministry. Through Jesus and His earthly ministry:

- The deaf heard.
- The blind saw.
- The paralyzed walked again.
- The woman with the issue of blood was healed.
- The centurion's servant was healed without Jesus even being present.
- Lepers were healed.
- The dead were raised.
- Demons were cast out of people.
- Jesus operated in the prophetic.
- Jesus received words of knowledge.
- Unusual miracles were done through Jesus.
- Money to pay taxes was found in the mouth of a fish.
- Jesus walked on water.
- Bread and fish were multiplied.
- Unexplainable catches of fish were recorded at His command.
- Water was turned into wine.
- Storms were silenced.
- Sins were forgiven.

The recorded ministry of Jesus was only about three years, but it made such an impact we are still talking about it two thousand years later. Jesus promised us that the works He did and even greater works would be done by us as we follow Him. The only qualification is that we simply believe. I love the way John concludes his gospel in summing up the ministry work of Jesus:

> *And there are also many other things that Jesus did, which if they were written one by one, I suppose that even the world itself could not contain the books that would be written. Amen.*
>
> —John 21:25

What an amazing heritage we have as followers of Jesus Christ! We have the opportunity to live absolutely remarkable, "eternity-shaping" lives—if we want to. The part that scares me is that we also can choose *not* to experience all God has for us as well. The power, authority, and gifts of God can also remain present but *dormant* in our lives if we choose not to exercise them. Another important ingredient God has provided to help us realize the potential He created us for is boldness. Boldness is something we all need, as it is required to walk in faith in what God asks us to do. The book of Acts illustrates the boldness that God gives us, as demonstrated through Peter and John.

> *Now when they saw the boldness of Peter and John, and perceived that they were uneducated and untrained men, they marveled. And they realized that they had been with Jesus.*
>
> —Acts 4:13

The simple act of being with Jesus caused Peter and John to be incredibly bold for Jesus. Praying for people and sharing our faith is often awkward, and it can be intimidating if we have not done it before. One of the things that really helped me to grow in boldness was to keep stepping out in faith. As I stepped out over and over, God showed up to help me with wisdom, power and gave me the right things to say. This experience proved that the same boldness He gave to Peter and John is available to all who fulfill the Great Commission. Jesus is faithful, and He can be trusted. I know this to be true both by faith in what He says in Scripture and in what I have seen Him do in response when I pray for people and share the Gospel. Through thousands of personal encounters, I have seen the truth of Scripture and His Word play out over and over and over.

In this book, there are many examples of the ways in which God moves and answers prayer. Greater still is the amazing work He is doing through petitions that occur unnoticed by us. There have been many times that I receive testimonies from people days, weeks and sometimes years later about what God did following a prayer. There may not have been anything sensational happening in the moment of the encounter, but the prayer proved to release the power of God into that person's life and brought healing and victory. I believe that only in eternity, when we fully know as we are fully known, will we have a greater appreciation for how amazing God truly is and what He did in and through us as we walked together through life.

The world around us desperately needs Jesus. *In a moment of obedience on our part and the sufficiency that God brings to the work He asks us to do, the trajectory of a person's life and eternity can be forever changed.* Depression can be broken, bitterness healed, marriages restored, and the list goes on. God is so capable that He can do more in a moment than we can do in ten lifetimes of our best effort. God has made this remarkable sufficiency available to each of us, and He has given us a mandate to use it to establish His Kingdom on earth as it is in heaven. This is both an exciting adventure and a tremendous responsibility. Our lives are but a vapor—here today and gone tomorrow. What will you do with the balance of your life? I challenge you to number your days and burn hot for Him. Know that you are deeply loved, and the saints who have gone before you are in the great cloud of witness cheering you on. Today is our day to shine for Him!

3

The Great Commission

And He said to them, "Go into all the world and preach the gospel to every creature."

—Mark 16:15

THIS PASSAGE of Scripture is also referred to as the Great Commission. The Great Commission is the greatest adventure we could be invited into. God loves us and the people around us more than we have the capacity to understand. This love is so great that He sent His only Son to die for us when we were still enemies of Him. The sacrifice of Jesus on that cross not only gives us eternal life, but it empowers us to live overcoming lives for the balance of our appointed days on earth. We don't have to go very far or look very hard to see how desperately the world needs the love of Jesus. We simply need to turn on the news, listen as we walk through the grocery store, or watch how people drive on the freeway. The world needs Jesus, and God has made accessing Him very simple. When I talk with fellow believers, I like to tell them we are incredibly rich. A relationship with Jesus is the most valuable thing we could ever ask for, without even a close second. Nothing compares to this. If it could be purchased, which it cannot, all the money in the world would not be sufficient to pay for all we have been given in Him. This priceless gift is ours to share with others, and we have it in limitless supply. This is so amazing when we really stop and think about it.

The Gospel is the best news ever—the news every person needs. Each one of us needs Jesus. All have sinned and fallen short of God's glory. There is nothing we can do in our own strength or ability to pay the price for our sins. The Bible tells us that the wages of sin is death. We are eternal beings, and the consequences of our sin without knowing Jesus as our personal Savior is an eternity in hell. God didn't want us to go to hell, which is why He sent Jesus to live a perfect life and then die a horrific death on the cross. When Jesus died on that cross, the punishment for all of the sin of all of humanity—past, present, and future—was poured out on Him. He bore it all, and paid the price for us. Jesus died and rose again on the third day, thereby conquering death. Jesus says that whoever believes in Him will have eternal life. This beautiful truth, also referred to as the Gospel, is what Jesus commands us to share with others so that all may have eternal life.

The command to share the Gospel is for all of us. The command is all-inclusive, and it applies to us all equally. Jesus did not qualify the command. Jesus did not say, "If you are a pastor, preach the Gospel." He did not say, "If you have been to Bible school, preach the Gospel." He did not say, "If you are a businessman, preach the Gospel." As followers of Jesus, we *must* share the Gospel and reach the lost. If you ask most believers, if they know that they are supposed to do this, and some do. If this is the case, why are more *not* sharing the Gospel?

The Good News of Jesus Christ is the key to our eternity and a fruitful life, yet it can be a challenge for us to share this Good News with others. I know this was the case for me in my initial years as a believer, and it is also the case for others. The reason for this varies from person to person,

The Great Commission

and I will cover some of the major obstacles in future chapters. The most important thing to consider now as it relates to sharing the Gospel is that *God knew* it would be a challenge for us. This is why He gave us spiritual gifts, as well as power and boldness, to carry out the work He has given us to do.

> *Now when they saw the boldness of Peter and John, and perceived that they were uneducated and untrained men, they marveled. And they realized that they had been with Jesus.*
>
> —Acts 4:13

This is one of my favorite passages of Scripture, as it gives us insight into what God knows about us and how He equips believers for the work we have been called to do. The mysteries of God are so vast that He knew we would need divine power and help to complete the mission He assigned us. How God works is very contrary to how the world works, and it is especially contrary to how our Western culture works. American culture is very dependent on experience and credentials. We hear from an early age it is important to go to college, get work experience, and work hard for a good life. While there is not anything inherently wrong with this philosophy, it can create a stumbling block for us to be used by God. We can create an obstacle for God that He never intended to experience. We can take our societal norms into our experience of being used by Him. We can put conditions on our being used, including in the realm of performance, experience, and credentials on ourselves or others to justify that we can't do it. If we feel like we are short in one or more of these areas, we may put off doing what He has asked of us until we address the gaps. This can result in years of inactivity for God in sharing His love and sufficiency with others.

God sees us totally differently than we see ourselves. God simply needs us to be available, to listen, and to be obedient. The rest of the "how" He *supplies.* In my experience, there is no pressure for performance or for us to flawlessly share the Gospel. When we have the childlike faith demonstrated by Peter and John, we will see God do the amazing. With God, we will operate in the miraculous. We will move in power and watch as God shapes eternity in our very presence. One of the reasons it is so hard to do is that it is usually awkward. If we are honest, we generally try to avoid all things that feel awkward. We prepare, we train, we study, and we come up with a plan so we know what to expect, what to avoid, and how to minimize awkward moments. This can be done to a degree in sharing the Gospel, but the greater portion is almost always *unscripted*. How people will respond, the questions they ask, and how God will orchestrate the encounter can vary substantially. This is where faith comes into the mix.

Even though Peter and John were uneducated and untrained by the standards of that day, God used them so powerfully that it caused the observers to marvel at them. It was apparent to those who observed that there was something miraculous and life-changing about being with Jesus. This was true *then*, and it is true *today*. Jesus is the same yesterday, today, and forever. This can be completely liberating if we let it. That same power that worked through Peter and John will work through you if you make yourself available. That same power will set people free around you from fear, sickness, depression, and addiction. God goes so far that He not only equips us, but He actually orchestrates interactions in which we can participate with Him in changing people's lives.

> *For we are His workmanship, created in Christ Jesus for good works, which God prepared beforehand that we should walk in them.*
>
> —Ephesians 2:10

When we see the truth of this Scripture play out in our lives, it is very inspiring and encouraging. Stepping out in obedient faith paves the way into availability as a lifestyle, we grow in our relationship with God, our understanding of how He sees us, and our realization of how He operates through us. As we turn our ear to His voice and do as He asks, we see the gifts He has given us develop, and we grow in Him as He radically transforms the lives of the people whose path we cross. If each day represents a page in the book of our lives, God is coauthoring a beautiful adventure story with us. As we walk with Him, life can turn from feeling monotonous to causing great anticipation of what we will see God do next.

> *How beautiful on the mountains are the feet of the messenger who brings good news, the good news of peace and salvation, the news that the God of Israel reigns!*
>
> —Isaiah 52:7 NLT

The path of the Great Commission is interesting and often unexpected in the way it plays out. I was once traveling for meetings in Northern California, and I felt like I should start my morning run at 5:30 a.m., which meant it was still pitch-black outside. My route took me by a completely dark park, but in the distance I could see the faint glow of a flashlight. I ran over to the light to find two men, whom I greeted and offered to pray for. One of the men declined and walked away. The other was a very large African American man who accepted prayer for addiction and his sexuality. The man marveled over the moving of the Holy Spirit in the prayer and the fact that I had approached him in such a way. He told me that people do not approach him in the light—and they definitely don't approach him in the dark! I inquired if he had a relationship with Jesus, and he did not, so I shared my testimony, including the Gospel, then gave him an invitation to accept Jesus. That man prayed to accept Jesus as his Savior right there in that park! He was so excited about Jesus and wanted to pray the same prayer with his kids. I left him with a copy of the book of John and told him what he needed to do next. I shared with him that he needs to pray every day, read the Bible, and find a Bible-believing church to get plugged into. The way to know if it is the right church is that he will have peace about it. One of the ways God confirms a course of action is through peace.

From there, my run took me through a forested area bordered by a high fence. I offered to pray for a man on the other side of the fence, who turned out to be a believer. However, he was greatly distressed about a $2,200 car repair and issues with his warranty. I prayed that God would break fear and anxiety off him, bringing peace, grace, and faith for an equitable resolution to the matter. The man was so encouraged and totally convinced that God had sent me, due to the timing, what he was going through, and that I had just appeared out of nowhere to pray with him.

A little later on during that run, I was crossing a parking lot and came across a young professional driving an Audi. I got the man's attention and inquired if he needed prayer for anything special. Since he did not have a specific request, I just prayed a blessing for him, his family, and his life. The Holy Spirit moved mightily in that prayer, and the man was greatly encouraged. I asked if he had a relationship with Jesus, and since he did not, I shared my testimony and the Gospel with him, then gave him an invitation to accept Jesus. That professional prayed with me to accept Jesus as his Savior right there in his car in the office building parking lot!

Experiences like this help to remind me about how sufficient Jesus is. While we all struggle with different sins, Jesus paid the price for all of them, and He desires that all would be saved. Each of these men were from different walks of life, struggling with different things, and they each were different in the degree of relationship they had with God. The encounters that morning were ordained by God; I believe He was pursuing each of those men. One of the things I am looking forward to in heaven is to learn more about people's stories. How was God working in their lives in the days, weeks, and months leading up to them giving their hearts to Jesus and their walk with Him that followed. Each person's journey is part of a divine plan that God is orchestrating. We may be planting a seed, we may be watering, or we may have a role in the harvest, but our participation is a choice. *There is freedom in this truth as it frees us from the pressure to perform.* All we need to do is listen to what God asks of us, whether that is to pray for someone, to share the Gospel, or to help in some other practical way. When we do our part, God takes care of the rest, and we will see eternity shaped through the course of our lives when we answer His call to reach those around us.

4

The Gospel

IN THE Great Commission, we are *commanded* to go and share the Gospel, or the Good News, with all men. This invites a natural question, which is: *What is the gospel?* Simply put, the Gospel is the message that we have forgiveness and eternal life in Jesus Christ.

> *For everyone has sinned; we all fall short of God's glorious standard. Yet God, in his grace, freely makes us right in his sight. He did this through Christ Jesus when he freed us from the penalty for our sins. For God presented Jesus as the sacrifice for sin. People are made right with God when they believe that Jesus sacrificed his life, shedding his blood. This sacrifice shows that God was being fair when he held back and did not punish those who sinned in times past, for he was looking ahead and including them in what he would do in this present time. God did this to demonstrate his righteousness, for he himself is fair and just, and he makes sinners right in his sight when they believe in Jesus.*
>
> —Romans 3:23–26 NLT

God loves us more than we have the capacity to understand. He wants a relationship with us, and He desires to walk with us through all of life's journeys, including the good, the tough, and everything in between. God wants to have a relationship with us, not only in this life but also throughout eternity in heaven. The truth is that we are all eternal beings and we will live forever. Only a small fraction of our existence takes place in this physical body. Even though God greatly desires a relationship with us, He is holy, and He cannot ignore sin. God is just, and justice must be served for wrongdoing. The reality is that each of us has sinned. We have all made mistakes. We have all fallen short. The truth of the matter is that there is nothing we can do in our own strength or capacity to undo or pay for our sins. People will lie to us and tell us that if we give money, that will compensate for our sins, but this is not true. Another lie that is popular is that if we do enough good works, it will make up for the bad choices we have made. If the good we do outweighs the bad choices we have made, then we will go to heaven. This, too, is a lie. The Bible says that the wages of sin is death. Hell was not God's plan for people. It was designed to punish Lucifer for his horrible disobedience. The devil's desire is to keep people ignorant of God's love and rebellious toward God. The claims of eternal justice require that we go to hell for our sins. Even though hell is what our sins require for justice to be served, God did not want that for us.

> *"For God so loved the world that He gave His only begotten Son, that whoever believes in Him should not perish but have everlasting life."*
>
> —John 3:16

God loves us so much that He sent His only Son, Jesus, to the earth. Jesus lived a perfect life without sin. Jesus went through a mock trial, was beaten mercilessly, had a crown of thorns placed on His head, and died a horrific death on the cross. Jesus died, but on the third day, He rose again. When Jesus died, the punishment for all of the sins of all humanity—past,

The Gospel

present, and future—was poured out on Him. After three days, God's requirement for justice had been fulfilled, and Jesus was raised from the dead. When Jesus was whipped, He paid the price for our healing. When Jesus took the crown of thorns on His head, He paid the price for our peace. Through His death, He paid the price so that we can have eternal life. The salvation that Jesus gives us cost Him everything, but He gives it to us as a free gift. There is nothing we can do to earn our salvation. The entire price for salvation was paid by Jesus. We simply need to receive this gift of salvation by faith.

> *The Lord is not slack concerning His promise, as some count slackness, but is longsuffering toward us, not willing that any should perish but that all should come to repentance.*
>
> —2 Peter 3:9

God loves us. God loves our neighbors, our coworkers, the homeless in our communities, the wealthy, the popular, and those who feel forgotten or marginalized. As the Scripture above clearly states, God desires that all would repent and receive the gift of eternal life He has provided in His Son, Jesus Christ. When we look at the world around us, we realize that not only does God desire us to be saved, but that we need a Savior. We all need the hope that is found in Jesus, not only for eternity, but for our day-to-day lives here on this earth. We need His grace, peace, wisdom, love, provision, long-suffering, patience, power, and all that comes with our relationship with Jesus. The book of Romans instructs us on how to receive the gift of salvation that God offers us:

> *If you confess with your mouth the Lord Jesus and believe in your heart that God has raised Him from the dead, you will be saved. For with the heart one believes unto righteousness, and with the mouth confession is made unto salvation.*
>
> —Romans 10:9–10

Of all the miracles that could take place, I believe the most significant is accepting Jesus and being born again, as this not only transforms our eternity, but it has the power to change our lives, families, workplaces, and even our communities. As we follow Jesus and His example, God will use us to encourage and strengthen fellow believers and to reach others for Jesus. How I share the Gospel can vary from person to person, but it largely follows the following pattern. I will typically ask if an individual needs prayer for anything or if they would just like a prayer of blessing for their life. Following the initial prayer, I will ask if the individual has a relationship with Jesus. If they already have a relationship with Jesus, I will encourage them. If they don't, I will share my testimony and the Gospel with them. Here is how I share my testimony and the Gospel with people.

The way I start my testimony is by telling folks I am going to tell them a story, which is actually my testimony. "I was raised Catholic and growing up, I literally went to hundreds of masses. This is not an embellishment, as I attended Catholic school, which involved attending mass, as well. I started off as a stubborn little boy, and do you know what I grew up into? A stubborn man. Even though I knew about Jesus, I did not have a relationship with Him. As soon as I was old enough, I left the church, and I had no intention of ever going back. I just partied, living life my way and on my terms, as years went by. Then, years later, a funny thing happened. I was in Portland, Oregon, on business, and I ended up in a church service. If you knew me at that time, you would have been very surprised by that development, as church was not "my jam." But I just sat in that church service and listened to that man talk. As he spoke, I realized that God just wanted to have a relationship with me, and one of us was making it real hard. It was not God who was making it hard; it was me!

The man also talked about the fact that God is holy and cannot ignore sin. The reality is that we have all sinned and made mistakes. I was no

The Gospel

exception to this truth. I had made many mistakes. If you were to have asked me to make a list of all the things I had done wrong, that list would have been so long, I wouldn't have been able to come up with it all. Even though I knew I had made many mistakes, however, there was nothing I could do to *undo* those choices. Through my own choices, I had earned a trip to hell, but God did not want that for me, which is why He sent Jesus to the earth. Jesus lived a perfect, sinless life, and then He died a terrible death on the cross. When Jesus died on that cross, the punishment for all the sin for all of humanity—past, present, and future—was poured on Him. The price for my sin and your sin was poured on Him. Jesus died and rose again on the third day. What God did next, however, blows my mind. Jesus died this terrible death, and then God lets us choose whether we want to receive this forgiveness or not. Friend, here is why this is important. You and I, we are eternal beings—we will live forever. Only a small part of our existence takes place in this body. One day our appointed days here on earth will be over, and we will step out of this life into eternity. The only way to heaven is through Jesus Christ. If we have a relationship with Him when we step into eternity, we will go to be with Him in heaven. If we decide that we don't want to have a relationship with Him or we make no decision at all, God will honor our choice, and if we step into eternity in that condition, we will spend eternity separated from Him, which means we will go to hell. This is very negative. God does not want this for us, and if you really think about it we don't want it, either.

I say all this to say to you that over twenty-five years ago, I prayed a very simple prayer. I told God that I would love to have a relationship with Him. I asked God to forgive me of my sins, and I made Jesus the Lord of my life. I asked God to help me in life. My prayer was simple and sincere. God heard my prayer and blessed every area of my life—my marriage, my kids, and my work. As beautiful as all that God has done for me, the thing I value the most is my relationship with Him. Friend, I have good news for you today. You don't have to go to Portland. You don't have to listen to that man talk. The same prayer I prayed all those years ago, we can pray together right now. It will be every bit as powerful and life-changing for you as it was for me. I can even give you the words, but the thing I cannot provide for you is your sincerity. Sincerity is the most important part of all. All you have to do is repeat after me and tie your heart around the words." I then invite the person I am sharing the Gospel with to pray the following prayer, and dear Reader, if you have not received Jesus as your Savior and you would like to, you can do it right now by reading the following prayer out loud with sincerity:

> "Dear Lord, I recognize that I am a sinner and need a Savior. I believe that Jesus died for my sins and was raised from the dead. I repent of my old way of life. I ask You to forgive me of my sins. I invite Jesus into my heart to be the Lord of my life. I ask You to help me to walk in Your ways all the days of my life. In Jesus' name, Amen."

When someone accepts Jesus as their Savior, I give them instructions on what they need to do next. The first thing I tell them is to pray every day. God desires to have a relationship with us, and talking with Him is a very important part of that relationship. The prayer doesn't need to be long or complicated; it can be simple, but it is important that we make that a part of our lives. Next, I encourage them to start reading their Bible every day. To help with this, I give them a copy of the book of John. I tell them that one of the ways God will talk to them is through His Word. I tell them they will be amazed as they read the Bible, that Scripture will come alive to them and apply to different areas of their life. I share that we have access to power, authority, and God's design for living a fruitful life, and that all that is found in the Bible. The other instruction I give them is to find a good, Bible-believing church. In the back of the book of John I hand out, I include the address, service times, and web address for

The Gospel

Cottonwood Church, and I invite them to attend an upcoming service. I also tell them there are many good churches out there, but that they need to be planted in the one God wants them to attend. The way you know you have found the right church is that God will give you peace about it. If you are uneasy about the church you visit, it doesn't necessarily mean it is a bad church or bad people; it is just God's way of telling you to keep looking until you have peace.

The reason you want to find a good church is that we all need community in our lives. Even though we have a relationship with Jesus, we will still have good days and bad days. All of us have been through battles, and we have valuable experience to share. God's economy works like this: You have something for me, and I have something for you. When we follow God's plan for community, each of us benefits from what the other person contributes. God has prepared a community for us to contribute to and benefit from. The other critical part of being planted in a local church is to learn more about God's Word so we understand what we have access to as followers of Jesus Christ and how we apply those gifts to glorify God and live fruitful lives.

If you have not already done so, I would encourage you to write out your testimony, including the Gospel, and practice sharing it. The construct of your testimony should be simple and consist of three parts. The first part is what your life was like before you met Jesus. The second part is how you heard the Gospel of Jesus and received Him as your Savior. The last part is what your life has been like since you received Jesus. The reason you should write it down is that this will help you to share your testimony concisely. You should aim to be able to tell your testimony in three to five minutes. Most of the time, the opportunity to share your testimony will take place while you are on an errand or in a location where the people you are talking to don't have the time for a lengthy conversation. By being prepared and concise, you will be equipped to reach people in a broad set of scenarios.

Sharing your testimony, including the Gospel, and giving an invitation to accept Christ is important for us as believers to do. We can and should invite people to church, but not everyone we talk with will go to church. Some who cross our paths may not ever have the opportunity to go to church following our interaction with them. People step into eternity at all ages and in a variety of ways. We may be providing the last opportunity some of the people we are talking with have to accept Jesus. We must invest the necessary time so we are prepared should the opportunity to share the Gospel with someone occurs.

The Holy Spirit will help you when the time comes to share the Gospel. He is ultimately the One who leads people into repentance and receiving Jesus. The more we practice this important discipline, the easier it will become. A good way to develop this skill is to go out with an evangelism team from church or someone you know who shares the Gospel regularly. Go with them on an outreach and see how it works in everyday situations. You can also read testimonies of recent encounters that I post to my website at tolmaoministries.org. This will help to prepare you for what to expect. The next step is to look for an opportunity to share your testimony and the Gospel with someone. This will take some courage, but you can be confident the Holy Spirit will be with you, guiding the conversation and giving you the right words to say. You will be amazed how God will use your availability in powerful ways. With practice, you will find that sharing your testimony along with the Gospel, then giving someone an invitation to accept Christ, is as simple as talking about your family or what you do for a living. As God uses you to bring people into a relationship with Him, you will be encouraged and develop a greater appetite to be fruitful and used by Him more often.

5

Rivers of Living Water

"But when the Helper comes, whom I shall send to you from the Father, the Spirit of truth who proceeds from the Father, He will testify of Me."

—John 15:26

ONE OF the promises Jesus gives us when we believe in Him is that He will send a Helper in the Holy Spirit. The Holy Spirit is so amazing in how He helps us navigate life and deal with challenging situations. He comforts us in disappointments, strengthens us in battle, and gives us wisdom in seemingly impossible situations. The Holy Spirit helps in every responsibility we have been assigned as followers of Jesus. This includes in marriages, raising our kids, managing our finances, and practicing ministry. The Holy Spirit no only works *in* us, but *through* us, as we fulfill the Great Commission.

"He who believes in Me, as the Scripture has said, out of his heart will flow rivers of living water."

—John 7:38

The promise Jesus gives us in this Scripture should give us great confidence in being available for Him to work through. This great equipping that God has given us provides tremendous power to transform the lives of people around us. This wonder-working power is available to do beautiful things in the lives of believers and those who do not know Him yet. The work of the Holy Spirit is effective in breaking chains, transforming lives, and shaping eternity.

One of the things I value greatly is the beautiful gift we have to see firsthand the truth of Scripture and to witness how God works in the lives of others. The power and gifts God has given us are truly remarkable, but they do not operate unless we choose to use them. We have the *choice* to use them or to let them remain dormant. We choose whether we will be like the Dead Sea, with great power flowing into our lives but not flowing out into the lives of those around us. The Dead Sea in Israel is without life because water flows into it, but not out. Spiritually speaking, our lives can be the same way if God's power flows into our lives but not into the lives of the people around us. The power of the Holy Spirit is meant to be like a river flowing *through us* to change lives around us and shape eternity. God gives us free will and desires that we would live fruitful and overcoming lives by being available to Him to work through. The more we seek God and step out in faith for Him, we will have greater revelation of how He works and how we can work with Him to encourage the body of Christ and see His Kingdom established on earth as it is in heaven.

Being available for God to work through is simple but not easy. Rarely do opportunities for availability come when we feel like it. The day-to-day demands of life rarely stand still so that we can be available for God. Most of the time you will be tired, in struggles, or frustrated about some aspect of life. Even though you will face your own limitations regularly, you can be confident that when you push through how you feel to reach others, the Holy Spirit will supply what you lack to bring what is needed in the lives of those whose paths you cross.

The power of the Holy Spirit is incredibly diverse, and how He works varies from encounter to encounter and from person to person. In my experience, people have described the Holy Spirit moving as follows: experiencing a sense of love, pins and needles, goose bumps, or peace, like electricity coursing through their body, like the urge to cry, feeling very good, or even uncontrollable weeping—and one woman reported smelling incense. The more frequently you make yourself available, the more you will see how He operates, and in turn, this will build your faith.

During some encounters, I have had people tell me what they are experiencing. Some of your learning will happen when you ask people what they experience after you pray for them. The most common way that I learn how God is moving is by asking people after I pray for them. I ask them, "Did you feel that?" Another question I ask is, "What stood out to you about that prayer?" Whether you ask or people volunteer to share, it is important that you listen and observe.

Romans 15:13 provides an example of how we can trust God to work through us regardless of how we feel:

Now may the God of hope fill you with all joy and peace in believing, that you may abound in hope by the power of the Holy Spirit.

—Romans 15:13

A good example of this occurred when I was traveling. On this particular day, I went for a run, and my rib was out of alignment. The pain was so intense I had to stop running. The day that followed was intense, and I was totally exhausted by the time I caught an early flight home. On the Uber ride back from the airport, I had a conversation with my driver, who was from the Middle East. He started talking about all the issues he had with the Bible. This was unusual, as I had not said anything about God, Jesus, or prayer at that point. During the ride, I shared that I had seen many miracles and went on to share testimonies of what I have seen God do. He told me he had pins and needles all over his body as I spoke. He shared that he had been talking with his mom, friends, and family members about his issues with religion the week before, and one of his family members had asked his mom why she let him talk that way. His mom told the family member that God would send someone to tell him the truth. Then he said, "Here you are!" I offered to pray for him, and he accepted. I prayed for this man, his mom, his dreams, and the business aspirations he had. The Holy Spirit moved in that prayer, and he was totally blown away. I shared my testimony and the Gospel with that man, and I gave him the invitation to accept Jesus as his Savior. He accepted the invitation, and I led him in prayer to accept Jesus as his Savior right in front of my house. Even though I was totally wrung out physically and emotionally, God was faithful in providing what was needed in that encounter to bring the hope and revelation the man needed in that moment.

Sometimes the Holy Spirit moves even before we start to pray. This happened one day when I was in a park near my house. A woman was walking nearby whom I felt like I was supposed to talk with, so I approached her and asked if she would like prayer. The woman requested prayer for her family and peace in their relationships. As I prayed, God led the prayer in the direction of peace and restoration of her relationships. When the prayer concluded, the woman gave me an unsolicited hug. Giving a stranger a hug is very unusual for me, but especially remarkable given the fact that I was completely sweaty from my run and did not smell the best. The woman went on to share that she had to fight back tears from the moment I began to speak to her. In this particular encounter, *I did not feel the presence of the Holy Spirit before or during the encounter.* However, just because we cannot feel God, that does not mean He is not moving. We just need to be available and trust that He is there and He will minister.

There are other times when the Holy Spirit will move and we can see evidence of His presence. This next story is an example of this.

Cottonwood Church was planning to do an outreach in our community through a local laundromat. The plan was to provide practical assistance by paying people's washer and dryer fees. Since I was organizing this event, I stopped by the laundromat to seek out the manager and ask if he was interested in us doing the event at his business. I asked one of the patrons if the manager was around, but he wasn't there. As I was about to leave, I felt God encourage me to go back and pray for the young man I had just talked with. I went back in and asked if he would like prayer for anything. The young man asked for prayer for work and his relationship with the mother of his child. The Holy Spirit moved mightily as I prayed, and the man wept openly. The moving of the Holy Spirit was so intense that there was a small puddle of tears on the floor by the end of the prayer. The goodness of God is such a holy thing to observe!

If we are willing to step out in faith and make ourselves available to God, we will see the Holy Spirit move in a variety of ways. This next example occurred when I was traveling. As I arrived at the airport to catch a flight, I was upgraded to first class. Once in my seat, I struck up a conversation with the man who sat next to me. If we are just friendly to those around us, we can learn a lot about people and where they may need help. The man shared that he was just returning from being in rehabilitation for substance abuse. This man was a designer, and he shared how he was a homosexual and had come out between the eighth and ninth grades. The man talked about how he had been searching for spiritual answers about the "higher power." We are all created with the desire for a relationship with God, even though we may try to meet that need with drugs, alcohol, or illicit sexual relationships. Ultimately, only a relationship with Jesus will satisfy this desire. I shared many testimonies of answered prayer, my testimony, and the Gospel with him. I told him *he could have a personal relationship with the God of the universe* rather than an impersonal acknowledgment of *a vague "higher power."* Then I gave him the invitation to accept Jesus. That man accepted, and I led him in prayer to accept Jesus as his personal Lord and Savior. I felt the Holy Spirit move as he prayed right there on the plane.

There were a few flight attendants serving our cabin, so I went up to see if they needed prayer for anything. One of the women requested prayer because she was missing her mother, who had passed away. The Holy Spirit moved mightily as I prayed that God would comfort her in her grief. Afterward, the woman told me that she felt very good as I prayed for her, and she gave me an unsolicited hug. The woman told me I was glowing. This was unusual feedback, but I have come to know that God is very personal in how people will encounter Him when we pray for them.

A little later, I asked the other flight attendant if she would like prayer for anything. This woman was mourning the loss of her twin, so I prayed that God would give her peace and comfort her in her loss as well. After I prayed for the second flight attendant, she reported feeling goose bumps as the Holy Spirit moved. She then asked for prayer for her mother, who was suffering with depression. I prayed that God would break that depression and give her peace. The woman reported feeling goose bumps again after the second prayer. I was struck that on the same flight, both flight attendants were mourning the loss of a loved one. God was truly amazing in the three divine appointments He orchestrated through an upgrade to first class!

The simple act of being available allows God to move. Living a life of faith and availability involves offering to pray for a total stranger, which is often awkward. Some people will say yes and others will say no. While rejection is never pleasant, the prize of seeing people comforted, encouraged, and set free is worth it, despite the potential awkwardness of the moment. The power of the Holy Spirit is more than enough for every encounter and situation. Have faith that God loves the people around you and that He can be trusted.

6

The Gifts of the Holy Spirit

THE HOLY Spirit has given us powerful gifts to live fruitful lives, to encourage fellow believers, and to fulfill the Great Commission Jesus gave us. Here is one of my favorite Scripture verses on the gifts of the Holy Spirit:

> *But the manifestation of the Spirit is given to each one for the profit of all: for to one is given the word of wisdom through the Spirit, to another the word of knowledge through the same Spirit, to another faith by the same Spirit, to another gifts of healings by the same Spirit, to another the working of miracles, to another prophecy, to another discerning of spirits, to another different kinds of tongues, to another the interpretation of tongues. But one and the same Spirit works all these things, distributing to each one individually as He wills.*
>
> —1 Corinthians 12:7–11

In the chapter that follows, I will provide a brief explanation of a few of the gifts referred to in this passage of Scripture that I see operate most frequently in my life. I will share some testimonies as an example of how they are used and how I have seen them impact people. The explanation that follows is not meant to be exhaustive, but it will provide insight as to what the gifts are and how they have helped me.

Each of the gifts of the Holy Spirit are very powerful and are applied in a much broader set of circumstances than the examples provided. As you study God's Word, apply what you learn, and make yourself available for God to work through, the Holy Spirit will give you greater insight into each of them and how they can be used for His glory.

The WORD OF WISDOM refers to an insight provided by the Holy Spirit. The word of wisdom can be for us or a challenge we are facing ourselves. Or the word of wisdom can be for someone we are talking to or are about to meet, regarding a challenge *they* are facing. The Holy Spirit is very active in the lives of believers, and this spiritual gift operates regularly. A word of wisdom can help us find our car keys, remind us to bring a tool to a job, or help us to repair something in a way that we could not figure out on our own. The word of wisdom comes to you as a thought related to the challenge you are facing. A simple example of this happened when I was repairing some landscape lighting for my wife. I couldn't find the wiring for a particular section of the yard, so I asked God to help me figure it out. A few minutes later, I had the thought to grab a three-prong root rake and move it through a particular area of the yard. As I did this, I found the wire I was looking for buried several inches below the surface. This saved me from hours of searching and aggravation. Again, this is confirmation that the more we ask the Holy Spirit for help in our lives, the more we will see Him aid us. This will help us to grow in our understanding of how He can help us or those around us.

Another example is a WORD OF KNOWLEDGE. This refers to an insight about a person or situation that we would have no knowledge of without the help of the Holy Spirit. God will use words of knowledge to highlight an area that may need prayer. He may provide a revelation to the person we are talking with that God is very aware of them and what they are facing. The Holy Spirit may reveal a health condition that was not disclosed in conversation, issues of anxiety or fear that someone is grappling with, or an insight into someone's profession or information about a trial they are going through. When we share a word of knowledge the Holy Spirit gives us with the person it was intended for, it is a great encouragement to that person. The insight builds their faith. The word of knowledge will also guide our prayer for that person. A great example of the power of a word of knowledge is given to us by Jesus in the book of John:

> *Jesus saw Nathanael coming toward Him, and said of him, "Behold, an Israelite indeed, in whom is no deceit!" Nathanael said to Him, "How do You know me?" Jesus answered and said to him, "Before Philip called you, when you were under the fig tree, I saw you." Nathanael answered and said to Him, "Rabbi, You are the Son of God! You are the King of Israel!" Jesus answered and said to him, "Because I said to you, 'I saw you under the fig tree,' do you believe? You will see greater things than these."*
>
> —John 1:47–50 NKJV

In this passage of Scripture, the Holy Spirit gave Jesus a word of knowledge about the location of Philip and what he was doing before Jesus met him. Nathanael was so struck by what the Holy Spirit revealed to Jesus that he believed Jesus was the Son of God. What the Holy Spirit did with Nathanael and Jesus happens today, as well. The word of knowledge, anointed by the Holy Spirit, captures the attention of those we talk to. This helps people to be receptive to what God wants to do in the conversation that follows. The conversation may serve to encourage them or provide an opportunity to share the Gospel.

Another gift of the Holy Spirit is the GIFT OF HEALING. I will touch on this gift here but dig into it further in the next chapter. The Holy Spirit will heal both *followers* of Jesus and *those who do not yet have a relationship with Jesus*. I have seen God heal people from many things, including medically untreatable migraines, vertigo conditions, organ pain, cancer, hearing loss, sprained ankles, and back problems. God's desire is that we walk in wholeness. Jesus took the stripes on His back so that we could be healed physically and emotionally. Healing is a very prevalent need in people's lives. Some people have obvious healing needs that are apparent by how they walk, a cast they wear, or some other indication of their condition. Other people need healing that is not apparent without asking them or receiving a word of knowledge from the Holy Spirit. The Holy Spirit will use healing not only to address their condition, but also to draw people into a relationship with Jesus.

The gifts of the Holy Spirit can operate through us one at a time, or we can see more than one of the gifts operate in one interaction. As an example, a friend of mine has a gift of healing and sees many people healed when he prays for them. The Holy Spirit will often give my friend words of knowledge about a condition that someone he encounters has. The person may have back pain or an issue in their neck. The Holy Spirit will tell my friend about their condition, and my friend will ask them if they are experiencing that issue. A key point concerning the word of knowledge is that faith is required to validate it. He must ask the person about the word of knowledge that he received for the person and whether they would like prayer for healing. If the person is open to prayer, my friend will then pray for them and will see God heal them.

The gifts of the Holy Spirit are for the profit of all. For much of my early life as a believer, the operation of the gifts of the Holy Spirit was limited to my life only. The reason for this was that I rarely offered to pray for anyone around me. I would pray for someone if they asked me to, but

The Gifts of the Holy Spirit

that rarely occurred. What I realized is that God does want to move in our lives, but He also wants to help the people around us. God does not force us to pray for other people. He has given us great power, but that power can remain dormant or be used in a limited fashion based on what we choose. We each choose how much we want to see God work in our lives and in the lives of others by how available we are willing to be for Him to work through. If we regularly offer to pray for those around us, we will see God answer prayer more frequently. What held me back was the concern over what other people might think of me if I offered to pray for them. When we offer to pray for someone, there is a very real risk that they may not be interested or reject us. This is a very normal concern, but it is one we must overcome if we want to see God do the miraculous in our lives and the lives of the people we meet. Over the years, I have learned that whether people accept prayer or not, stepping out in faith is required to make an impact in the lives of other people.

This reminds me of a story of two individuals I encountered one morning when I was out for a run in my city. Early in the morning, I came across a man walking, and I stopped to ask him if he would like prayer. The man quickly and gruffly declined. I have found that sometimes people decline prayer before they really understand what I am asking them. We live in a society that is always trying to sell us something, so we have been conditioned to say no when someone offers us something, even if it is a legitimate gift. Just to be sure, I asked the man a second time if he was sure he would not like prayer. The man then got angry with me about how persistent I was and had some other choice words for me. Even though I faced total and complete rejection, I continued to run, looking for the next person whom God wanted me to talk with.

My route that morning had me returning on the same road I had departed on, which had a large senior living facility on it. As I passed, I noticed there was a man and a woman sitting and talking on their porch.

When I inquired whether either of them needed prayer for anything, the man said he had great pain in his legs. I prayed for that man, that by the stripes of Jesus he was healed, and that Jesus would heal his legs and the pain would leave. After I was done praying, I asked the man to stand up and do something that had hurt him before. I asked the man that, if the pain level had been a ten when I had approached him, what was it then? I asked him to tell me the truth and not say his legs were better just to make me feel good. The man walked a bit and began to marvel, telling me the pain level was now a six. I prayed for him again and told him to test it one more time. The man reported the pain level was at a four. As I left, I encouraged him to keep standing on the promises that God would complete the healing He began.

About three weeks later, when I was on another run, I saw the woman again and greeted her. She was happy to see me and told me about how the two of them had been talking about me and the miracle the man had experienced in his legs. I find it so interesting that in the same city, on the same day, on the same patch of ground, one man got angry and another man received a miracle from God! This still serves as a powerful reminder to not get caught up in the negative responses, but to simply be obedient to what God asks, trusting Him to work out the results. If I had let the man who was negative cause me to quit taking risks for God that day, the man and woman and I would have never seen the healing miracle that was to take place!

The way in which God moves always makes me marvel. God orchestrates divine appointments with incredible precision in the most unexpected ways and places. I was in Reno, Nevada, and I went for an early morning run while it was still dark out. As I made my way through the city, I was struck by the grip of addiction and homelessness all around me. I was surprised by the number of people wandering the streets at that early hour. As God directed me through the streets that morning, I came across a Chevy Impala parked in the middle of the road.

The Gifts of the Holy Spirit

As I approached, I saw two men covered in tattoos unloading electronics out of the back of the car. Undeterred, I inquired whether they would like prayer for anything. The men smiled and gave each other a look like, *This guy is crazy*, but they accepted prayer for their lives. I prayed for them, for God's plan for their lives, and for their identity in Him. As I was praying, I had the distinct impression of someone invading my personal space. I turned around to find an elderly man looking directly at me. I concluded the prayer with the other two men and then asked the elderly man if he would like prayer for anything. The man just nodded so I suggested we go over to the sidewalk to pray, as we were standing in the middle of the road.

The man asked for prayer for healing related to his hearing. I realized the man's hearing was severely compromised, which is why he was so close to me when he was communicating with me. By the stripes of Jesus, I prayed that this man would be healed, that he would experience the radical love of God and all that God had planned for him. As I prayed, the man's eyes became very large, and then he began to cry. When I finished praying for him, the man asked who I was, as he could now hear me clearly. God had healed this precious man's hearing right there on the sidewalk. I asked him if he had a relationship with Jesus, and he did. I told him that Jesus had just healed him. All glory to God! The man then shared he had an appointment later that morning to have his hearing aids adjusted and that he wasn't sure what he was going to do about it since he no longer needed hearing aids!

God had lined up three very distinct encounters at an appointed time, in the midst of this city with so many other things going on. These encounters serve as a good reminder that God has worked out the who and the how, and He will orchestrate the location and the conversation. All we need do is be listening for His instructions and be obedient in what He asks us to do. God takes care of the rest. We get the benefit of a front-row seat to His marvelous works!

As we follow Jesus on the Great Commission, we will face rejection from time to time. Jesus was our example, and He faced rejection regularly. If He faced that, how much more will we face it as we follow His commandment to take up our cross and follow Him? Rejection comes in many forms, ranging from our just being ignored, to some rolling their eyes, to others claiming to be atheists or agnostic, and the list goes on from there. Regardless of what we encounter when fulfilling the Great Commission, we must persist, because many beautiful encounters await us as we persist in the work of the Father. We must not be dissuaded by the "no thanks" response we will get at times.

The next encounter is an example of the Holy Spirit giving words of wisdom and knowledge. I left my house, following a simple set of instructions of where to go. I came across a man who was walking south, and I felt like I was to approach him. When I spoke to him to get his attention, he looked at me as if he knew me and gave me a heartfelt thank you for taking him to the hospital. This caught me off guard because I did not recognize him. He went on to say that I had saved his life. Still confused, I listened as the man continued to share that he had recently spent thirty days in the hospital. The man had been shot by a .22-caliber gun, the bullet had been lodged in his kidney, and it had caused a massive internal infection that he did not know about. As he said these words, I remembered the encounter I'd had with this man months prior.

The man and I had originally met near a local train station. He had been in a lot of pain and had requested prayer for healing. I prayed for healing for him. He did not recover immediately after the prayer. Following the prayer, I felt an immediate conviction to walk him to a nearby hospital. The conviction I experienced was a word of wisdom. The man and I walked to the hospital, then entered through the nearest entrance, and the staff at the front desk insisted we leave and go to the emergency room entrance. The emergency room was all the way on the other side

The Gifts of the Holy Spirit

of the hospital and would have involved two to three long city blocks of walking. I had a conviction that the man must be received there, however, so I insisted that they take him in and transport him to the emergency room. After some back and forth, the hospital staff finally listened and brought a wheelchair to transport the man. In the month that would follow, God would use those doctors and that hospital to bring healing to that man. God had spared this man's life, and I told him that God had done so for a reason—because He has amazing plans for him. While the world may count us out, God does not. He is sufficient to turn our situation around, redeem lost time, and bring lasting fruitfulness out of our availability. That man had been living on the streets for seven years, and God had good plans for him to give him a future and a hope.

There are times when God gives us a word of knowledge that will require us to step out in faith without a specific confirmation. During a mission trip to Kenya, I was walking on the beach and saw a woman in the distance sitting on a log. The word "peace" came into my mind. As I approached her, I inquired if she would like prayer because God had put her on my heart regarding a matter of peace. She did not disclose what she was struggling with, but I told her it was okay because God knew her situation, so I prayed over her as the Holy Spirit led. She acknowledged His presence, and I explained to her what she was experiencing. I asked if she had a relationship with Jesus, and she did not. The woman told me she was searching but still had many questions. I smiled and shared that questions are good and God Himself gave us our inquisitive minds. I went on to share my testimony, along with the Gospel, then gave her an invitation to accept Christ. The woman said she was not ready to accept Jesus; she was rooted in questions and wanted to know if God was a woman. I told her to seek God in her quiet time, asking Him about the importance of a relationship with Jesus and what to do about it. When God speaks, she should do as He leads her. I implored her to take the matter seriously because it is the most important decision she will ever make, for the only way to heaven is through Jesus. I wished her well and continued down the beach. When I got to the prayer rock that had been off in the distance, I turned around and came back. As I made my way back up the beach, I could see her in the distance walking away from me, but then she stopped and sat down. As I approached her again, I asked, "Christine, are you ready?" She paused, thought a moment, then nodded and stood. She accepted Jesus as her Savior that morning—all glory to God! As I walked back, I thought about the beautiful work of the Holy Spirit, who was actively working before I arrived, as I spoke, and in the time from when I left to the time in which we spoke again. These encounters serve to help me trust that God is at work regardless of what may happen in any given interaction, and that He truly is drawing those He loves to Himself.

The stories I just shared are examples of the Holy Spirit moving to heal as well as give wisdom, a word of knowledge, and the necessary boldness to act. You may have a sense of the gifts God has given you. If you do not, digging into the Bible and studying the life of Jesus is a great place to start. Ask God what spiritual gifts He has given you, and He will tell you. Your gifts will be revealed by what you have a heart for and are drawn to. As you ask God to give you an opportunity to be used by Him and step out in faith, you will see a pattern forming in your life regarding how God reaches people through you. The more you use your gifts, the more you will see them developed and have greater wisdom in how to use them to help those around you.

7

Healing

Surely He has borne our griefs and carried our sorrows; yet we esteemed Him stricken, smitten by God, and afflicted. But He was wounded for our transgressions, He was bruised for our iniquities; the chastisement for our peace was upon Him, and by His stripes we are healed.

—Isaiah 53:4–5

THE BOOK of Isaiah, written approximately seven hundred years before the birth of Jesus, foretold of Jesus and all that He would do for us through His redemptive work on the cross. The life of Jesus modeled how we are to follow Him. The same Jesus who was healing people two thousand years ago is still healing people today. Healing ministry is available for all of us. What is required is faith—a willingness to stand on the promise that He is able and willing to heal. In the book of John, Jesus instructs us that if we believe, the works He did and greater we will do because He has gone to be with the Father. The earthly ministry of Jesus demonstrated remarkable miracles of healing. The blind saw, the deaf heard, the woman with the issue of blood was healed, and those with terminal illnesses were healed. One of the most insidious and feared diseases of that time was leprosy. The Gospels record accounts of Jesus healing many of leprosy. The paralyzed walked, and the list of all He did was so expansive that John concludes his gospel by saying that "If every work that Jesus did was recorded in books that perhaps even the world itself could not contain the books." What a heritage we have as followers of Jesus and all that we can look forward to if we are simply available for Him to work His healing power through us.

This topic could be an entire book. There are many great books that dig deeply into this subject. For the sake of time, I will share just a handful of testimonies where I have seen the healing work of Jesus in the course of my day-to-day life. The first story came about as I was taking an Uber to the airport. As I like to do, I struck up a conversation with my driver, and the conversation included me sharing some testimonies of some of the beautiful miracles I have seen God perform in the lives of people. I mentioned how I met people dealing with fear, vertigo, insomnia and unforgiveness, and how God had helped those people. The driver told me that she had been involved in a major accident when she was six years old, and she'd had to learn almost all aspects of living. As she drove, she shared that she had been struggling with debilitating migraines since that time; they were so bad she was now on medical leave. She had been to many doctors, and they had performed many tests on her, but they came back inconclusive. None of the prescribed treatments worked. The woman shared how she was struggling with jealousy in a current relationship, suffering from insomnia, and was still struggling with abandonment issues from her father leaving her when she was one year old. I shared my testimony, including the Gospel, then gave her an invitation to accept Jesus as her Savior. She prayed with me to accept Jesus as her Savior while we drove to LAX. I then added a prayer for healing, peace, and the promises of God for her life. Amazingly, she told me her headache left as I prayed for her. The issue of her father and the unforgiveness that she had discussed weighed heavily on my heart as we drove. I talked with her about the issue of unforgiveness and the importance of forgiving her father. I shared that forgiving him was most important for her, as it was necessary for her to be truly free. She said she was willing to forgive him as she wept openly. We prayed that Jesus would help her forgive him, so that she could release him and be set free. God did a beautiful and deep work in that precious woman on a simple drive to the airport.

When we are available for God to work through, I find that He arranges opportunities. The key is to be intentional, be available, and *listen* for where people need help. An example of this took place when I was traveling and stopped by Starbucks for a quick breakfast. The store was crowded, so I asked another customer if I could share her table. We talked, and she shared that she taught photography to troubled youth. During our conversation, she mentioned that she was suffering from an abdominal issue that the doctors couldn't diagnose or treat. I shared testimonies of healing with her and offered to pray for her. The woman accepted, and I prayed that Jesus would heal her. Upon the conclusion of the prayer, the woman reported an immediate improvement in her condition!

This particular day, however, God had more in store for me. God heals in a variety of ways, and there are times when He moves in ways we do not expect. On my second flight of the day, I was seated next to a woman from Ireland. Since the flight was long, we had a fair amount of time to talk, so I shared testimonies about the goodness of God. The woman shared how she struggled with fear, anxiety, unforgiveness, and a major condition with her liver. I offered to pray for her, and she accepted. I prayed for her healing and spoke the promises of God over her life. When the prayer concluded, the woman shared that when I prayed for her, she felt like her liver was being cleansed and washed out as I prayed. For the balance of the flight, the woman remarked multiple times about how much better she felt. God truly is amazing in the healing work He does when we ask Him. He is so willing!

Many miracles have occurred in the gym where I work out. The following story is an example of how God moved in a several different places. My routine is to warm up in the Jacuzzi before beginning my swim workout. I once offered to pray for a lady who was in the Jacuzzi, but she said no, stating that she was a Buddhist. I told her that God loves Buddhists, and I shared a few testimonies of two Buddhists who had been healed in that very gym. She thought about it and then accepted, so I prayed the love and promises of God over her life. I asked her if she felt that, and with a very large smile, she said "yes." A woman who was in the pool behind us then chimed in that she had felt it too. The woman in the pool went on to say that what she saw was so beautiful and pure that it was like rivers of living water. What a surprise it was that she was listening! It turned out that she was a believer, too, and was encouraged by seeing God work in the gym.

I changed and went to do my strength and core work out. I noticed a man who was stretching out on the mat next to me. He winced as he moved, and I knew he had major back pain, as I had suffered from chronic back pain for many years before God healed me. I told him my testimony of healing and asked if he wanted prayer. He accepted, and we prayed right there in the midst of many other people working out in the area. I spoke the love and healing power of Jesus over him by the stripes He took (Isaiah 53:4–5), commanded the pain to leave, and asked Jesus to heal him. I then asked the man to test it out. The man moved around and confirmed that the pain had gone from a ten to a six. I prayed again, and the man was surprised. He began stretching and twisting, and I could tell by how he moved that God was healing him right there. He confirmed the pain was almost totally gone, now at around a pain level of two. I told him to be expectant as God was going to finish the healing He started, as it was an expression of His love for the man.

Healing

As illustrated in the previous examples above, I like to ask people how they feel after the prayer. If they were experiencing pain and that is what we are praying for healing for, I ask them to test the area of their body we are trusting God to heal. I ask them to tell me the truth and not to tell me they feel better just to make me feel good. If the condition is the same, they should tell me so. If it is better, they should tell me that. I ask them, if the pain level was ten when we first started talking, what is it now? I typically see God move in a few different ways. The person may experience no improvement in their condition. If they don't experience improvement, I tell them to stand on the promises of healing and that I do see healing occur sometime after the initial prayer. The person may experience an improvement. If this is the case and time is permitting, I will pray again to advance the healing. If not, I tell the person to stand on the promises and believe that God will finish the healing work He started. The third scenario I see is that the person may be totally healed in the moment. This is always my hope and preference, but how and when God heals is entirely up to Him. He knows what is best, and I just trust Him in how He chooses to work.

Another routine I have is running. One day I was getting ready to run, and I had an impression of a parole bus. There is a park about a mile and a half from where I live that is in a pretty rough part of town, where a bus would pick up parolees. God didn't give me any insight other than that thought, but that was enough for me to go on. I set out running to where I knew the bus picked up the parolees. On my way to the park, I crossed paths with a woman who was walking, and I asked her if she needed prayer. This woman went on to explain that she had a tumor in her back that was causing ongoing chronic pain. I prayed the healing power of Jesus over her and His promises for her life. When the prayer concluded, I asked her how she felt. The woman shared that God had brought an immediate improvement in her condition, describing it as heat that started in the upper part of her back that traveled down her left arm and out of her body, bringing relief as I prayed. I simply prayed, and God brought the healing relief in a beautiful way.

There are times when God will prompt us to pray for healing, but we may not see anything in the moment. A little later on that run, I saw a different lady and just had the thought of healing. I politely approached her and told her what God put on my heart. She told me that she did, in fact, have some sort of abdominal condition that she was very worried about; she was having medical tests soon concerning the issue. I prayed the healing of Jesus over her and that she would have peace that He was going to heal her. There was not a report of an immediate improvement that day. I have seen God heal people sometimes days, weeks, and months later on many occasions. I trust that God will complete what He started in that conversation.

When I got to the park, the parole bus was there. This was confirmation of what God had put on my heart, since I did not know the schedule of the bus or if it would even be there at that time. I asked the police officers in charge if it would be ok if I prayed for the folks on the bus. The officers agreed to let me pray for the group, and one of the officers requested prayer for himself. The other officer specifically asked that I pray for the six new people on the bus. I asked the people on the bus if they had any specific prayer requests. Two people requested prayer for their moms, and one had a request for an uncle with an addiction problem. God led the prayer using the story of Joseph in Genesis, and God's ability to redeem us from the most impossible circumstances. The Holy Spirit swept through that van, and one of the women wept openly as God comforted her.

As we step out in faith to answer God's call and lead, He will prove Himself amazing. He will use us for His specified purpose. As I walked away from the parole bus, I saw two men at the other side of the parking

Healing

lot. The men were just standing in the parking lot, and one of them had a very large, menacing-looking pit bull on a leash. The dog did not appear to be remotely friendly, and it growled and barked at me as I approached. I offered to pray for the men. They were initially very cold to the idea but eventually accepted. As I began to pray, they removed their hats and bowed their heads, and the dog stopped growling and barking and simply laid down. One man remarked that even his mom didn't pray like that for him. I shared my testimony, including the Gospel, and gave them an invitation to accept Christ. By this time, the formerly angry dog was now curled up, lying at my feet. Both men accepted my invitation and prayed with me to accept Jesus as their Lord and Savior. God not only brought peace to that dog and protected me, but He also did a beautiful work in the hearts of those two guys whom He loves so much!

The park where this all took place is regularly filled with homeless tents, drug addicts, the mentally ill, and is regularly in our city's police blotter for a variety of crimes that take place there. As desperate as the place is and the people who are found there, God loves them. Jesus died on the cross for each of them, and He wants to see them healed, forgiven, and set free. Where darkness abounds, grace abounds more. What is so beautiful about God is that we can see Him move powerfully in places just like this—and our own neighborhoods, as well—if we are simply available for Him to work through. The price of admission is asking awkward questions and facing rejection. This cost is trivial compared to the price that Jesus paid on the cross and what God will do through our obedience. Through our availability, we gain a better appreciation of God's love toward people and the lengths He will go to in order to save and restore them. This helps us to understand how great God's love is toward us as well and reminds us that He can be trusted and is always more than enough regardless of what we face or how impossible a situation may look in any given moment.

8

Hearing from God

Therefore I also, after I heard of your faith in the Lord Jesus and your love for all the saints, do not cease to give thanks for you, making mention of you in my prayers: that the God of our Lord Jesus Christ, the Father of glory, may give to you the spirit of wisdom and revelation in the knowledge of Him, the eyes of your understanding being enlightened; that you may know what is the hope of His calling, what are the riches of the glory of His inheritance in the saints, and what is the exceeding greatness of His power toward us who believe, according to the working of His mighty power which He worked in Christ when He raised Him from the dead and seated Him at His right hand in the heavenly places, far above all principality and power and might and dominion, and every name that is named, not only in this age but also in that which is to come.

—Ephesians 1:15–21

HEARING FROM God has always been a topic that has intrigued me, and it continues to be one I pursue. God has helped me a tremendous amount in this area, and it is one in which I continue to grow. As believers and followers of Jesus Christ, it is vital that we are intentional in seeking

God in all areas of our lives. This is especially true as it relates to ministry and the good works that God has prepared for us to do. Without His guidance, it would be impossible to know what He has planned for us and what we need to do so He can effectively work through us. This is a very deep topic, and the thoughts that follow are not meant to be all-encompassing. They are simply some thoughts that have helped me learn to hear from God. My hope is you will find something here that will help you grow as well.

For a long time, I wanted to hear from God but was convinced that I didn't or that I rarely heard from Him. What I found is that the more often I was intentional about sharing the love of Jesus with people, the more I would hear from God. Hearing from God is just like learning to play a sport. *The more you practice, the more skilled you become.* Jesus is our ultimate example because He only did what the Father asked Him to do. When we live our lives with the intention of sharing the love and sufficiency of Jesus with those around us, we will not only see God do beautiful things in their lives, but our relationship with God will grow. As our relationship with God gets stronger, we will be more attentive to the multitude of ways that God speaks to us.

One of the most important disciplines that I developed is becoming a student on how God communicates with people. I learned by studying the Scriptures, listening to sermons, hearing testimonies from other believers about how they heard from God, and then how God communicates with me when I am doing outreach activities. God communicates to us through images, impressions, Scripture, or lyrics to a worship song. When we ask God if there is anyone He wants us to talk to in a crowd, we may notice someone wearing a particular color or have a thought about someone that is standing next to us. Other clues can be a thought about a vehicle or a landmark where we are located when we ask. While those descriptions may be broad, *as we develop the discipline of availability*, we will learn to recognize how God is directing us.

One of the ways that I learn best is through real life examples, so I am going to share some different testimonies of how God has instructed me and what happened in those encounters. A common theme that you will see in each of the examples is *they were all awkward and required stepping out in faith.* With each encounter, there was the possibility that I got it wrong or that the person would not be open. *It is critical not to let such thoughts or possibilities stop us from being used by God.*

One of my favorite things to do is surfing. One of my favorite places to surf is in Hawaii because the water is warm and the waves are great. I was traveling on business once in Hawaii and had some time after work to paddle out for a workout and some fun. Since it was the end of the day, the only place I could get to before dark was Waikiki. If you have ever been there, you know this is largely a tourist surf spot, but there are some locals who frequent the break. As I paddled out, there was a large Pacific Islander who stood out to me among the crowd waiting for the next wave. God told me that He loved that man and that the man came out there to find peace. I knew I needed to talk to him.

This was a bit of a tricky encounter as he was an incredible surfer and seemed to catch every ridable wave. There was eventually enough of a lull in the waves, however, that I was finally able to paddle up to him to share what God had put on my heart. The man just looked at me stoically, but he seemed thankful. We continued to surf without any further interaction, until God put the man on my heart again. This time, I had the impression that he was being tormented, and that if I prayed for him, God would set him free. Even though it was awkward, I paddled up to the man again and started sharing testimonies of what I had seen God do. Sharing testimonies from friends, our personal experiences, or what we have read in the

Bible is very important as it helps to build faith in the person to whom we are talking. As we were talking, we caught a current that pulled us 75 feet away from his friends and the other surfers. I offered to pray for him at that time, and he accepted. I prayed the love, liberty, and promises of God over that man. When I concluded, I asked if he felt it, and with a giant smile, the man confirmed feeling the Holy Spirit move in the prayer. I left a different man than I had found in the lineup that day.

The traffic in southern California is pretty rough, and parking at the airport can be scarce, so I often find myself taking Uber to and from the airport. This has proved to be an incredible way to minister to people. One evening, I was returning from a trip, and I took an Uber home. The female driver and I had a conversation that found its way to talking about God and the amazing things I have seen Him do. The woman went on to share with me more of her personal story. She had just come out of a really rough patch, as she was a single mom who had gone through a period of homelessness. Thankfully, God helped her find a place to live, and she was driving for Uber full-time. But she still had been struggling with depression and anxiety. As she spoke, God put on my heart that it was time for her to dream again. I shared this with her and asked her about her dream job. The driver told me that she loved design and wanted to remodel homes. She accepted prayer for her future, so I prayed the promises of God over her life. The Holy Spirit moved mightily in that prayer, and she wept deeply as He brought peace, comfort, and hope. As the prayer was coming to a close, we turned onto the street that I lived on. As I said "amen," the most amazing thing happened. Even though it was dark, the night sky totally lit up, as if to put an exclamation point on the prayer. The event was so remarkable that she stopped the car and we tried to figure out what it was. I later learned it was SpaceX sending a satellite into orbit, and I still marvel at the incredible timing and encouragement it brought to both of us that night.

Hearing from God

Another way I have heard from God is by seeing an image of someone. This happens very rarely for me, which is why I still vividly remember when it occurred. I was driving to the gym and praying that God would use me that morning to reach people. I asked if there was anything that God had for me that day. The next thing that happened was an image of a man from the gym flashed in my mind, bringing with it a deep conviction about the state of his soul. The man was someone I recognized but knew very little about. I just instinctively knew that I needed to share the Gospel with him as soon as possible. When I arrived at the gym, I went looking for that man, but I could not find him. I completed my swim routine and then headed back to the gym for strength and core work. This time I saw the man, and so I walked directly over to him. He was doing burpees at the time, so I waited for him to finish. Once he was done, I told him that God put him on my heart, and I went on to share my testimony and the Gospel. I gave that man an invitation to accept Christ, and he accepted. We prayed together, and that man accepted Jesus as his Lord and Savior right there in the middle of the gym.

God can also talk to us about people when we see them and challenge us in unexpected ways. These "calls to action" are rarely convenient, often coming at inopportune times. I was traveling for business and heading to dinner one night. Indian food is one of my favorite cuisines, and I was going to a restaurant that I liked. As I was looking for a parking place, I saw a homeless man who was very dirty and walking on the sidewalk. The thought immediately came to mind to invite him to dinner with me. The day had been long, I was tired, and I was in no mood to be stretched in this way. All I wanted to do was just grab a quick meal and go to bed. Nevertheless, I parked the car and went looking for the man God had spoken to me about. After some searching, I found the man two blocks away, walking in the wrong direction, so I had to run to catch him. Once I caught up to him, I asked him if he would like to join me for dinner. The man accepted and turned around to walk with me. As we walked, I shared what God had put on my heart, including my testimony and the Gospel. As we were about to enter the Indian restaurant, the man asked if I could just buy him some pizza instead, and I agreed. The man was so happy, as he had not eaten in two days. I bought him pizza, he accepted Christ, and I prayed a prayer of turnaround over his life. Even though I was tired and not in the mood, God had ordained a beautiful encounter and an eternity-shaping moment for me on the way to dinner that night.

There have been times when God has spoken in a variety of ways all in the same day. One morning I had the hope that my day-to-day life would come together so I could focus on what God called me to do. As I was having this aspiration, the image of a homeless camp came into my mind with the conviction that I needed to go there. This was not an assignment I was particularly happy about, as it was a very large encampment and it was in a place where there were no streetlights, so it was likely to be completely dark. The challenge was amplified by the fact that the rain was driving very hard in the city I was in. These are the moments when we need to choose His will and not our own.

As I set out for the homeless camp, God took me the long way, and as always, it was with a purpose. There was a man waiting at a bus stop who accepted prayer for his life. The timing turned out to be absolutely perfect. As I said "amen," the bus doors opened, and he stepped in and was off to work.

As I ran into the homeless camp, I noticed a man in the shadows standing outside in the rain. *I greeted him and asked if he needed prayer for anything.* The man asked for prayer for a turnaround in his life, his marriage, and his identity in Jesus. The Holy Spirit moved mightily in the encounter. The man was greatly encouraged as I had appeared out of nowhere and the Holy Spirit rocked his world. The man in the tent next to him also gladly accepted prayer, marveling at the encounter as the leak in his tent was the only reason he had come out. Once again God had prepared multiple encounters, in succession, and all with perfect timing. On my run back, I prayed for three professionals in three different cars. Each person confirmed the move of the Holy Spirit. Once I got back to the hotel, I showered and headed off to work.

As I waited to board my plane later that day, I heard a man talking on his mobile phone about giving a legal testimony, being interviewed by the media, and some other business issues. The man ended up sitting next to me on the plane. I was totally exhausted due to my day and quickly fell asleep. As the plane approached its landing, I was awakened thinking about the man and night terrors or nightmares. There wasn't any additional information about what it meant or what I was supposed to do with the information.

Even though it made me uncomfortable, as we approached the baggage claim, I said hello and engaged the man in conversation. After some initial comments, I found out he was a medical doctor by training and the CEO of a company. I shared that God often speaks to me about people, and I inquired about him having nightmares. He said that typically no, he didn't have them, but he was totally honest when he admitted he'd had a very rough night the night before and could not sleep. God had given me an accurate word of knowledge. I offered to pray for him, but he declined, stating that he was an atheist. Even though it appeared that the interaction hit a dead end, I am confident that God is using that interaction to draw that man closer to Him.

Another way God talks to me is by giving me the desires of my heart. In this particular case, I was going to dinner, and I felt like I should go look at tools at Sears. This was very strange, as I was in a different city and an airplane flight away from home. Nonetheless, I parked the car and walked into Sears. In the tool section of the store, I saw a young man, whom I greeted and engaged in conversation. I asked if he would like prayer, and he accepted prayer for his life. I shared my testimony and the Gospel with that man, and he accepted Jesus as his Savior right there in the tool aisle. As I left the store, I crossed paths with another man on the way to my car. We talked, and he accepted prayer as well. I asked if he had a relationship with Jesus, and he did not, so I shared my testimony and the Gospel with him. That man prayed with me to accept Jesus as his Savior right there in the parking lot of the mall. God is so remarkable in how He plans encounters for us and then leads us into those engagements in such a variety of ways.

God will use others to talk to us and encourage us as we are learning to be used by Him. I have had this happen so many times, I have actually lost count. One example occurred when I was in Hawaii. I was going to grab a quick lunch before heading to the airport. In the restaurant, I noticed three people sitting at a table. One of them was in a wheelchair, another was in a walker, and a third person was accompanying them. I walked over to see if any of them needed prayer for anything, and they requested prayer for healing and life. I prayed over them, and all were thankful. As I went to sit down, a man and woman approached me and wanted to know my story as they were in ministry and have never seen anyone pray for a table of strangers in the middle of a restaurant before. We had an amazing conversation over lunch, sharing stories of what we had seen God do. I asked if they wanted prayer; the woman wanted prayer for healing, and the man needed peace. After I prayed, they reported feeling the Holy Spirit move, and the man said that peace had just washed over him as I prayed. They both prayed and prophesied over me as well, confirming many things that God and others had spoken over me. They gave me Psalm 91, which has been a *rhema* Scripture for me, which was very powerful. God spoke powerfully to me through that couple in ways they could not have had any previous knowledge of. God had orchestrated a beautiful exchange in that restaurant, both for me to pour into others but also to have others pour into me.

There are times when God's communication to me is a very simple thought. One example of this is from a trip I was on. My day was just about over, and I needed to get gas for the rental car. There was a gas station near the hotel I was staying at. One of the men working there had accepted Christ on a previous trip. I had the thought to get gas and see how he was doing. When I walked into the convenience store, there was a woman at the counter who was telling the clerk that she had a craving for a cigarette but she didn't really want one. I told her that if she wanted to be set free from that desire, I would be happy to pray for her. I went on to explain that I consistently saw God do the miraculous. As I was talking, the Holy Spirit fell, and the woman began to cry. She said she saw God all over me and that I was an apostle. The man working behind the counter confirmed what she said and told her that I had prayed for him too.

The woman went on to share that her grandson had just been admitted to a psychiatric facility, and she was distraught about it. God had put it on her heart to make peanut brittle even in her distress. This woman made and sold peanut brittle. The man working at the gas station loved her peanut brittle and was one of her customers. God had perfectly orchestrated the paths of our lives to converge at that moment, and then He showed up in radical fashion. As I prayed, the Holy Spirit moved wonderfully. God will move in the most amazing ways and in the most unexpected places if we simply listen and obey. That beautiful encounter could have just as easily not happened for a host of reasons. The woman could have stayed home in her distress, I could have blown off going to see that guy because I was tired, the man could have stayed home from work, or there could have been any other multitude of reasons. When we consider it, the chances of these encounters not happening is exponentially more than the chance of them occurring. In spite of the statistical impossibility, however, God orchestrates them over and over. The sufficiency of God is truly a beautiful thing to behold, especially when you see all He does through such subtle communication.

My hope is that the experiences that I have shared are helpful in illustrating a few of the ways God talks to me and what happens when I step out in faith to reach people. God is not a respecter of persons, what He does for me, He will do for you. Just like all disciplines, it is important that we are intentional in hearing God's voice and stepping out in faith. We simply need to listen, do what He asks, and He will respond. We simply need to listen, and He will respond. There will be times when we may get it wrong or a person may not be receptive to our approach. My encouragement would be to keep at it. God is found when we diligently seek Him. He is the perfect Teacher. The other thing that is important is to find a friend with whom you can share your experiences. You will be surprised at how much sharing testimonies will encourage you and others. As we are faithful in this discipline, we will see God move in greater and more frequent ways. I look forward to hearing about the great exploits *you* will experience walking with the King of kings and the Lord of lords!

9

Divine Appointments

STEWARDSHIP IS very important to God in all aspects of our lives including our marriages, raising our kids, managing our finances, and in carrying out the great commission. God is so wonderful: He not only prepares good works for us, He has prepared *rewards* for us for the good works He has prepared.

> *For we are His workmanship, created in Christ Jesus for good works, which God prepared beforehand that we should walk in them.*
>
> —Ephesians 2:10

This passage of Scripture is one of my favorites. This carries not only wonderful opportunity, but also great responsibility. Since God has created us for good works, and has even gone so far as to prepare good works for us to walk in, it is critical that we are obedient to do what He has asked us to do. How we steward what God has prepared for us matters a great deal to Him.

> *And whatever you do, do it heartily, as to the Lord and not to men, knowing that from the Lord you will receive the reward of the inheritance; for you serve the Lord Christ.*
>
> —Colossians 3:23–24

God wants us to be *doers* of His word and not just hearers. When Jesus commands us to follow Him, we are to follow His example of how He lived His life. Jesus proclaimed the Kingdom of God, He healed the sick, and He did the Father's will. Jesus operated in the prophetic, spoke words of knowledge, and performed unusual miracles. The example Jesus gave was followed by the apostles and in the life of Paul. Where did these happen? Not just at church gatherings but in the streets and in people's homes. God desires us to follow the example of Jesus. He has equipped us for the work and has orchestrated the good works for us to walk in.

In the accounts that follow, I will share a few examples of divine appointments I have experienced that have been orchestrated by God. My hope is that these testimonies will encourage you to seek Him diligently about where He wants to use *you*. It is important for all of us to seek the gifts that God has placed in us and how we can use them for His glory. In the parable of the talents, God shares His heart on the importance of not letting our gifts stay dormant, but that we should use them to help others and to bring glory to His name.

One Sunday, Pastor Joel brought a brilliant message on how God sees people very differently than we do, with our limited perspective. Looking at people through our natural eyes may lead us to the conclusion with some that they are on our "probably not" list of likely candidates to accept Christ. This is why it is so important for us not to judge but to simply be obedient to what *God* asks us to do and trust the Holy Spirit to do the rest.

A trip I took to northern California later that week would illustrate the truth of what Joel preached about. I was in town for a meeting and woke up early for my customary run. I had an impression on what time to start my run and the direction to run in, and I found myself going a very long distance through a residential area without seeing anyone. In fact, it was so long that I completely lost my sense of direction and soon had no

Divine Appointments

idea where I was. After running a couple of miles, I finally came out of the neighborhood and found myself near a gas station. I felt impressed to go over to a car at a gas pump, but there was no one in it. The car at the next pump had a man standing outside the vehicle and a woman in the car. When I asked if they want prayer, the man accepted, as he was homeless and currently living in his car. As I prayed for the two of them, I noticed a large hammer and battery-powered angle grinder with a metal-cutting disk on the floor of his car. I wasn't judging, but if someone was going to steal catalytic converters, those would be the perfect tools to use. As I finished the prayer, both confirmed feeling the Holy Spirit. The man later shared that this happened to him regularly. I was the fifth person to have prayed for him in the last two months. This made me a little jealous, as I have never had someone approach me and ask me if I would like prayer! I asked if he had a relationship with Jesus and he did not, so I shared my testimony, including the Gospel, and gave them both an invitation to accept Christ. The man and woman both prayed with me to accept Jesus as their Savior in the early morning hours at that gas station.

God had orchestrated a beautiful divine encounter for that couple with absolute perfect timing. If I had arrived just a few minutes earlier, they would not have been there. If I had arrived a few minutes later, they would have already gotten their gas and been on their way. God is remarkable in the precision of the divine encounters He orchestrates.

The diversity of God's divine appointments are very broad, and there are times when He will orchestrate them to teach and encourage us. God's timing in the most intricate details of the encounters is remarkable. I find the timing of Uber rides to be particularly noteworthy. The moment we request a car, the request goes out, and we are then paired with a driver. Requesting the car a moment earlier or a moment later will result in a pairing with a different driver. Even though there is no margin for error for the appointment, God orchestrates them with perfect precision. This next story is an example of this.

I was traveling to Virginia for a meeting and took an Uber to my hotel. I struck up a conversation with my driver who was a very interesting man, originally from Iran. The guy was a self-described "man's man"; he was very driven, he had served in Vietnam, and he was a big-game hunter. The man had been raised as a Muslim, but he shared that he hadn't been very religious for most of his life. About ten years before, he told me he had been diagnosed with two kinds of cancer, which resulted in him undergoing an operation for both cancers at the same time. While he was under anesthesia, he said that Jesus visited him in a dream and let him know that He died to save him. He just wept as he described Jesus. He went on to share how God had spared his life on multiple occasions, and how this opened the door for him to have the relationship with Jesus he had that day. The only way to describe this experience was holy. The man did accept prayer for his health, and he was encouraged by the prayer. As I reflected on the night, I felt like I was the one who walked away truly blessed after hearing about how Jesus had visited this man in a dream, how Jesus had saved his life, and how Jesus can capture the hearts of even the toughest among us.

There are times when God will arrange divine appointments on the other side of opposition and rejection. When we conduct our outreach nights, it is very common for the early parts of our efforts to be marked by significant rejection. Despite the rejection we will undoubtedly encounter, it is critical that we persist in faith to reach the people that God has sent us to. One evening we had an outreach in Huntington Beach, and we were sharing the love of Jesus at the pier. I was handing out tracts and offering to pray for people. This particular night roughly fifteen people in a row told me no and refused to engage in any conversation with me. The next person I offered to pray for was a young man who had been raised as a Mormon; he was curious about my road to Damascus. The concept of grace was totally intriguing to him. I shared my testimony, including the Gospel, as well as the promise of living an overcoming life with him. He shared his previous religious experience and his personal situation in which he had made a mistake and engaged in sex before marriage. He desired to get his life right. He shared that the process that "religion" had given him to receive forgiveness was to go before twelve men, to share his sin in detail, and to leave it up to them as to whether he would receive forgiveness. He followed the instruction and shared his story with these men, who would ultimately determine if he was truly sorry and if he could be forgiven. After thirteen months, the group was divided—six voting for his forgiveness and six voting against it. The process he went through ended up costing him his relationship with the young woman. And in the end, the men from whom he sought forgiveness did not forgive him, as they were not convinced he was truly sorry. This story literally made me want to vomit. I was so moved by this young man and the fact that even though "religion" had been so awful to him, *he* was still seeking God. He loved the idea of grace. He asked about the rules I believed in. I shared that we needed to love God with our whole mind, heart, and soul, and love our neighbor as ourselves. On these, all of the other commandments were hung. The young man took notes as we talked. He was so hungry for the Lord. In the end, I led him in prayer to accept Jesus as his personal Savior right there at the pier. As I told my wife the story in the morning, I just wept. It was such a precious and beautiful experience to be a part of. God is amazing, and while there are plenty of people who are not ready, there are those precious souls who are hungry and are searching for someone to share the authentic love of Jesus Christ with them.

God is so precise that He not only accounts for where people will be, but also how long each conversation will take and the travel time between encounters, and He can line things up even to meet a train schedule.

While I am not a statistician, I would venture to guess the probability of the timing of the events randomly happening in sequence is as close to zero as you can get. This is why I believe God does not share all that is in store since it would be totally overwhelming for the human mind to process. The encounters that follow are an example. But first, I am going to share many interactions that led up to the story I want to highlight. These examples will demonstrate the level of orchestration that God used leading up to an encounter with a precious couple and how God concluded the series of encounters.

I was on a business trip in Salt Lake City and felt like God had something in store for me there after work. I didn't have much to go on, so I simply left the hotel and waited for direction from God as I walked. God directed me as I walked through the city, and I prayed for a few friends who were talking in the plaza. I also met a street evangelist who shared testimonies about many things, including how he had seen someone raised from the dead. I prayed for him for greater influence, anointing, and works of God in his ministry, and he prayed a powerful prayer of impartation, favor, and grace over me. Later, I met and prayed for a man for a place to live; and a man in front of a tattoo shop. Next, I prayed for a man walking on the street, a man at a bus stop, and a man walking around the park. The next person I prayed for was a man who was going to prison the next day and looked afraid and hopeless. The Holy Spirit moved powerfully, and this man's countenance changed. He was so thankful.

Further on there was a library in the city with large, sprawling grounds where a large number of homeless people congregated. I had no prior knowledge of this library or the number of homeless people present, but God had led me there on my walk. In this area, I prayed for three young homeless people sitting by the sidewalk; prayed for three homeless adults sitting on some stairs as the Holy Spirit moved. The next opportunity for prayer came with a group of more than ten homeless people who surrounded me in a stairwell. As I prayed, more people came and joined the group. The Holy Spirit shifted the atmosphere, bringing peace, hope, and comfort to them. All were thankful for the encounter. After that, I prayed for another group of eight who were initially closed to my words, but God changed their hearts during our conversation. This is why I am politely persistent when I engage people, to give the Holy Spirit time to soften hearts. We had a rich conversation, and the Holy Spirit moved through my prayer for them. Following this encounter, I also prayed for a young couple who had been fighting while they were celebrating their anniversary. The Holy Spirit washed over them, and both wept as they were both encouraged and comforted. I then had an opportunity to pray for a man with dreadlocks for freedom from substance addiction. The Holy Spirit moved in the prayer, and the man gave me an unsolicited hug. I prayed for a couple who was packing up their camp. I prayed for three young people for their identity in Jesus and gainful employment. Following those encounters, I prayed for a young man on the street and for a man standing at the entrance to the library. The next person I prayed for was a young man who experienced the Holy Spirit powerfully. I shared the Gospel with him, but he was not ready to accept Jesus as his Savior.

Across the street from the library was a train station, which is where I felt I was supposed to go. I crossed the train tracks to the station. There was a tall African American man with dreadlocks on the train platform who coldly accepted my offer for prayer. The Holy Spirit moved mightily in that prayer, and the man hugged me and kissed me on the cheek when the prayer concluded!

As the interaction with this man concluded, a train stopped and let off more than twenty people. In the crowd of people who got off the train, a young couple stood out to me. Since God put them on my heart, I approached them and asked them if they needed prayer for anything. The couple skeptically accepted prayer for their lives, but they did not have any specific requests. I prayed that they would experience the authentic love of Jesus, that they would be filled with the fullness of God, and that they would have a breakthrough in a number of areas in their lives. As I prayed, the Holy Spirit moved mightily, and I watched as their countenances changed, they drew closer together, and they wept as they experienced the love of God. When the prayer concluded, they marveled, wondering why I had approached them. I told them that God loved them and had sent me to them. I asked if they had a relationship with Jesus, and they did not, so I shared my testimony, including the Gospel, and I gave them an invitation to accept Christ. That couple prayed with me to accept Jesus as their Savior right there on the street!

I continued walking and soon came across a young man who accepted prayer for his father, who was depressed. The Holy Spirit moved in that prayer, and the young man was thankful. As the encounter ended, I suddenly realized I was right back in front of my hotel. This was remarkable to me, as I had just been walking as God prompted, but I had not been keeping track of where I was in the city. God had totally orchestrated the encounters and the route, even bringing me back to my hotel. Adventures like this with God are truly amazing. God had opened the door for fruitful ministry in an unexpected walk that took just a couple of hours. He provides the power, the words to say, the directions, the protection, and He brings the results. While I didn't record those who said no on this particular day, the walk was certainly punctuated with those who wanted nothing to do with me or prayer—*but I don't allow that to deter or discourage me*. Our role is simply to be available to God, not be distracted by the rejection and to be intentional about praying for those that are open.

The good works that God has prepared for us will vary by the day. Some days He may have someone for us to pray for. Other days, He will ask us to encourage a friend or help someone with a practical need. Other days, God will do something special for us or use a friend or stranger to encourage us. Our responsibility is to pay attention to God and have an inquisitive heart to ask if there is anything He would like us to do. The more intentional we are about listening for His voice, the more we will hear His voice. As we are obedient to what He asks and step out in faith, we will experience great encounters that will bear fruit that will *echo into eternity*.

10

Waiting on God

Therefore judge nothing before the time, until the Lord comes, who will both bring to light the hidden things of darkness and reveal the counsels of the hearts. Then each one's praise will come from God.

—1 Corinthians 4:5

THIS IS such a beautiful passage of Scripture, but it runs so counter to our culture. Waiting can be very difficult, especially when we are fulfilling what God has asked of us. This discipline is extremely important as we only observe a fraction of what God is doing in the lives and hearts of those who cross our paths. Our role is a small part of what God is doing, but there are times when God will reveal more of what He is doing to set people free and draw them into freedom and a relationship with Him. The stories that follow are a few examples of what I have seen God do that required patience, but brought great fruitfulness.

One night I arrived late at a hotel, and I struck up a conversation with the night manager as I checked in. Through the course of our conversation, I shared a number of testimonies of answered prayer and inquired if she would like prayer for anything. Just then, a large group of pilots and flight attendants came to check in. The manager was interested in prayer and told me she would call me when she finished checking everyone in. As I left to go to my room, I felt the impression that I needed to go back and talk to her in person. I went to my room to drop off my belongings and to wait. After some time, I felt the urge to go back to the lobby. After she had checked in the last of the flight crew, we went and sat down in the lobby to continue our conversation.

This woman shared that she had been suffering from a deep depression, and she felt like she was at a crossroads in her marriage. As we talked, she would periodically comment that she was very private and focused only on business at work so she couldn't believe she was sharing this with me. She went on to share that she was attracted to another man who was not her husband, and she needed to know what to do. God directed the conversation in such a beautiful and powerful way. I told her that she wanted me to tell her to leave her husband for the other man, but instead she needed to stay with her husband and that the other desire was a lie from the pit of hell intent on destroying her. She also shared that she was in terrible bondage from unforgiveness for a mistake she had made and had suicidal thoughts. The thoughts had become so severe that she was actually making plans to end her life. I shared many testimonies of answered prayer and how God can redeem us from the most impossible situations. I prayed over her and the many challenges that she had shared. The Holy Spirit moved mightily in that encounter, and the woman's countenance totally changed as I prayed. I shared the Gospel with her and gave her the invitation to accept Christ. That night manager prayed with me to accept Jesus as her Savior right in the lobby of that hotel. The woman I left was different than the one I had met when I first arrived! God did such a beautiful restorative work in our time together even though our conversation was initially interrupted.

Waiting on God

For we are to God the fragrance of Christ among those who are being saved and among those who are perishing. To the one we are the aroma of death leading to death, and to the other the aroma of life leading to life. And who is sufficient for these things?

—2 Corinthians 2:15–16

One experience comes to mind that illustrates the importance of waiting and patience. The pool was down at my gym so I went to an alternate gym in a different part of the city. After my swim set, I went to the sauna, which was packed. There were a number of men there, and I offered to pray for them. One man accepted prayer for pain in his neck, one for his life in general, and the other six had no specific requests and didn't seem particularly interested. As I prayed, a few other guys filed in. Upon concluding the prayer, I had the thought to ask if anyone needed to accept Jesus, so I asked the question. No one responded; they just looked at me. I went on to share testimonies and the Gospel with the men. As I spoke, one of the men engaged with me, and I asked if he would like to accept Christ. As I was about to lead him in prayer, one of the other men asked us to step outside as he was trying to relax. The man who wanted to accept Christ had ten minutes left in his sauna session, so I told him that he was important and that I would wait. Waiting for ten minutes might not seem like much, but it sure feels awkward in the moment. After waiting ten minutes outside the sauna, the young man finally stepped out, and I led him in prayer to accept Jesus as his Savior. I found it interesting that this Scripture explains what happened in the sauna that day. While some may be uninterested or even negative, there are still people around us who are hungry for the truth, and God is drawing them into a relationship with Him. When these opportunities present themselves, *it is important that we are willing to wait through the awkward moments to see God move.*

Another story of waiting on God took place when I was traveling. After I had dinner, I was browsing at a local bookstore, and I had the impression that something was waiting for me. The day before, I had received a coupon for a free dessert at the hotel next to where I was staying. When I arrived, the restaurant was almost empty, so I sat at a table in the middle of the restaurant after ordering apple cobbler. The waitress was from the Philippines, so I shared many great testimonies from ministry work that we had done there. I shared my testimony, including the Gospel, and I gave her an invitation to accept Christ. The woman accepted, and as we were about to pray, her manager called her away. The woman was gone for a very long time, so it felt very awkward to just sit there and wait, but I did. After what seemed like an hour, she finally returned, and I led her in prayer to accept Jesus as her Savior. While the process took longer than I would have expected, God had a plan.

There are times when waiting on God can span months rather than minutes. This next testimony is an example of how I had the opportunity to participate in more than one aspect of a man's salvation journey. As an effort to reach our local community, we had arranged to pay people's washer and dryer fees at a local laundromat. Even though we had a big team on-site, the number of patrons that came that day was low. This gave me the opportunity to talk with the manager. While we were talking, I asked him if he needed prayer for anything. The man asked for prayer for unity in his family and his life. As I prayed, the Holy Spirit moved and touched this man deeply. When the prayer concluded, the man looked at me as if he knew me. He told me that I had prayed with him before. He went on to share that he'd had many people pray for him, but my prayer with him was very different, which was why he remembered me. He refreshed my memory that it had been many months prior; I had prayed with him and his brother in front of a restaurant that his brother worked at. As he described the scenario, I remembered the encounter. I asked the man if he had a relationship with Jesus, and he did not, so I shared my testimony, including the Gospel, and I gave him an invitation to accept Christ. That man prayed with me to receive Jesus as his Savior right there in the laundromat. When I gave him instructions on what to do next and gave him a book of John, he recognized it. He told me they give you those when you are in prison. This encounter served as a great reminder that even if people tell us no, God is still working in their lives and will use others to draw them into relationship with Him. *We just need to be faithful in the assignments we are given* and ultimately trust God for the outcome.

There have been occasions when people flatly reject offers of prayer and want nothing to do with the Gospel but God will still use us to plant a seed that will bear fruit later. One example of this took place with a man I ran into in the sauna one day. The man was a big, well-built guy with tattoos. As I entered the sauna, he told me "I want you to know that I was wrong." At first, I did not recognize him. He shared that I had offered to pray for him over a year prior and he had rejected the offer. At the time, he said he told me that "all he needed in life was my health." The man went on to share that when I'd talked to him initially, he'd had a major alcohol addiction, and he would come into the sauna just to dry out. In the time since our first encounter, he'd come to realize he did need God after all, and he now had a relationship with Jesus. While I had nothing to do with the events that followed, the man vividly remembered our conversation, which appeared to me to be a total rejection. How great is that? Never underestimate what God does through our obedience, even when it appears to be a total failure! *The name of Jesus is above every name . . .* and every "thanks, not interested." For everything that we see, there are countless examples of what God is doing behind the scenes that we will not see until eternity. This is why it is so important for us to be diligent and available for God. Celebrating the victories and the breakthroughs that we see is important to do. More importantly, is to be obedient in what

God has asked us to do when we don't see the breakthrough or victory. God's Word does not return void, but it accomplishes that which He sends it to do. When we face rejection, it is critical that we stay "on mission" and resist the urge to give up. We need to trust that God has a plan and will use other workers to accomplish that plan, especially in matters that involve rejection or waiting. God will order our steps in the positive encounters, those that require waiting, and even the rejections. Another way to think about the rejections is that the person is simply telling us "not yet." That is when we hand the baton back to God and trust Him to work out the rest and His timing for their life.

11

Rejection

> *"Blessed are you when men hate you, and when they exclude you, and revile you, and cast out your name as evil, for the Son of Man's sake. Rejoice in that day and leap for joy! For indeed your reward is great in heaven, for in like manner their fathers did to the prophets."*
> —Luke 6:22–23

REJECTION, OR the fear of rejection, is one of the most common obstacles to believers fulfilling the Great Commission. Not liking rejection or fearing the possibility of rejection is a *normal* feeling we *all* experience. As followers of Jesus Christ, we must push through this to do what He has asked us to do to reach a lost and dying world. *The more active we become in reaching people for God, the more irrelevant rejection is.* There is no silver bullet besides walking it out. The first time we get a "no" or a dirty look when we talk to someone about Jesus, it stings quite a bit. I used to mull it over on how I could have engaged that person differently. If we don't quit and keep going, though, the next time it is easier. Over time, I concluded that any rejection is just a manageable part of the process.

People will say "no" in a variety of ways. Some will politely decline. Some people will ignore you. Some people will roll their eyes. Other people will use profanity. Some will share how they have another faith, which could be Buddhism, Islam, atheism, agnosticism, a belief in Mother Nature, Hinduism, science, or even Satan himself. I have heard all of these and more. When I share testimonies with fellow believers, some folks are most encouraged by the stories of rejection as they are so easy to relate to. God is absolutely amazing in that He actually brings fruit out of rejection. Here are a handful of examples that illustrate how He does this:

There have been many marvelous moves of God in the gym where I work out, but not everyone is positive or even open to prayer. There are folks who are happy to see me, and some who will actually come ask for prayer when they see me. The opposite is also true, as some people will immediately leave when I walk into the sauna! Others are just not open, or they could be mildly negative. There was a particular woman who was very cold to my offers of prayer for her or to anyone else. One day I was in the sauna and asked if anyone needed prayer for anything, and this woman was in the group. Much to my surprise, she did have a prayer request—for her grandma, who had recently had a stroke. The request was not kind or even nice, but I didn't let how the request was packaged bother me. I prayed for the group and for her grandma specifically, that she would recover from her stroke. The following week, I was back in the sauna. There she was, and this time, her attitude was totally different. She sincerely thanked me for praying for her grandma. The lady's grandma was recovering from her stroke, eating again and just as feisty as ever. Encounters like this remind me that I need to be bold for Jesus even in the company of those who are closed or negative. We never know when God is going to turn the situation around.

The other risk of allowing rejection to stop or slow down our reaching the lost is that we can't see what happens next. One example of this came

Rejection

when I was traveling. I had just finished dinner and was about to leave the restaurant to go back to the hotel. As I was leaving the restaurant, I had the impression that I needed to go to Starbucks. While I was there, I offered to pray for both of the people working there, but neither of them were interested. Once I had my coffee, I went outside and sat down at a table. A woman walked by with a cast on, and I struck up a conversation with her. As we spoke, I shared testimonies of how I had seen God heal people, set people free from fear, and come through in the area of finances. She did not have a relationship with Jesus, so I shared my testimony and the Gospel with her. She was not ready to accept Jesus, but she was open to prayer. I prayed over her life, that she would be healed in her foot and that she would be set free from fear. The woman reported describing what felt like a weight coming off her while I prayed. I encouraged her to sincerely seek God on the matter of Jesus and what she needed to do. She said she would, and then she was on her way. When I reflect on that series of encounters, I am reminded that any of those people who said no could have derailed that woman's victorious experience if I had let the disappointment of the moment convince me to stop. There are times when people can be very negative, but I have seen God do beautiful things, even with very "salty" people. Overcoming disappointment is critical, not only for what God is doing in that moment, but for what could be in store in the interactions that follow.

This next story is a good example of God doing the surprising even in the face of rejection. I was in traveling in Baltimore, and it was in the fall, so the morning temperature was very brisk. My usual routine is to go for an early morning run prior to starting my day. On this particular morning, God led me down by the water. As I was running, I came across a homeless woman who was outside under some blankets. I inquired as to whether she needed prayer for anything, and she asked for healing as she suffered from chronic pain. While I prayed that God would heal her physically and turn her situation around, a man startled me by jumping out from the blankets and briskly walking across the street. When the prayer concluded, I asked the woman how she felt. Just then, the man returned, and I asked him if needed prayer for anything. The man aggressively declined prayer, punctuating his communication with profanity. The man explained how bad his tooth hurt and that he didn't want prayer. I simply asked God to heal that man's abscessed tooth as a reflection of His sufficiency and love toward this man. I then asked the woman again how she felt. As soon as the woman shared that she noticed her condition had improved, the man told me his tooth no longer hurt. God totally surprised me in that He healed a man who not only had declined prayer, but who had done so with extreme profanity!

Little did I know, but this was just the beginning of what was going to unfold in the day ahead. Farther in the run, I came across a woman at a bus stop who asked for prayer for healing as she was suffering from flu-like symptoms. After I prayed for her, the woman reported an immediate improvement in her condition. At the same bus stop, two homeless men were behind a glass enclosure, with one of them so sick he was doubled over, constantly coughing and sneezing, and his nose was running so bad he couldn't even talk. I prayed for those men, for their lives and that the sick man would be healed. Nothing happened in that moment, but when I returned after running a seven-mile loop, both men were standing there, totally fine. The man who had been sick appeared to be completely healed; he was not coughing or sneezing, and his nose had stopped running! Later in the run, I talked with a Hindu man who seemed totally indifferent to prayer, but I prayed for him anyway. The Holy Spirit rocked his world so profoundly that he literally gave me a hug afterward as he explained how impactful it was. There was a Whole Foods store on my path, where I offered to pray for a woman who was very skeptical but who accepted prayer. I prayed for her marriage and finances, and the Holy Spirit moved

Rejection

mightily as she wept. That woman gave me an unsolicited hug, as well. Then, on my flight home, I had the impression that I should talk to the flight attendants. There were three of them who accepted prayer, although one was extremely skeptical. God did something very special in that prayer, as the countenance of the skeptical one totally changed during the petition. That previously skeptical flight attendant shared it was the most incredible prayer she had ever heard. I told her that what she experienced was a hug from God, who loves her so much. It was so cool!

On my home from the airport, I shared many healing testimonies with my Uber driver, who told me he was getting goose bumps as I talked. He accepted prayer willingly, and I prayed boldness over him, that he would be filled with Holy Spirit and that the remainder of his life would be marked by walking in the miraculous and everything that Jesus had died on the cross to accomplish. When the prayer concluded, he just slumped over the steering wheel in his car. We were in front of my house, thankfully. The man described the experience as similar to being connected to live electricity and that he had never experienced anything like it before. I love the Holy Spirit and His amazing ministry! God truly had beautiful things in store for me on the other side of that rough rejection that I had encountered at the beginning of my day!

Experiences like this can remind us that the cost of letting rejection overly influence us can not only cost the person we are talking to, but also come at a high price for those who will cross our paths later in the day. There are times when God will literally turn around someone who is initially negative. This next example happened when I was out for a run in a neighboring city near where I live. I was running on a major arterial road, and I suddenly felt like I was supposed to cross all five lanes and go down a residential block. I did so, and two houses in, I noticed a man in the driveway with a reciprocating saw. I asked him if he would like prayer, and the man was very quick to shut me down with an emphatic *no*. He went on to share that his brother was a Jehovah's Witness, and they were always coming by to proselytize. I laughed and told him that it sounded like they were after him. This broke the ice, and he walked over and we just talked. He shared how he had been at the hospital for an appointment for his wife, and when he was in the parking lot, he saw a woman fall down, and he went over to help her. When he went to lift her up, there was the sound of a *pop* in his back that, resulted in both of them needing help. When I learned about this injury to his back, I asked if he would like prayer for healing, and he *did*. I prayed over him, for his back and for his wife's health. When the prayer was over, I asked him to test out his back. I told him that if his back didn't feel better, he shouldn't lie to me just to make me feel good. If it was better, though, I wanted to know that too. If his pain level was at a ten when I'd approached him, what was it now? He told me that his back had been hurting when I came up, but it did get better after I prayed. I asked if he had a relationship with Jesus, and he did not. I shared my testimony and the Gospel, and that man accepted Jesus as his Savior right there in his driveway. God used laughter and the Holy Spirit to break up the negativity in the moment, in order to bring healing to that man and open his heart to the Gospel.

God has an amazing adventure planned for you. Rejection is part of the adventure. If they rejected Jesus, they will certainly reject us. We can strongly dislike it, but we must also follow the example of Jesus and endure it. In the moment, it may seem unpleasant, but those feelings quickly dissipate after you obey the Lord, leaving you with a deep sense of gratitude that God helped you be obedient to follow His example in reaching the lost. As you persist in this important discipline, some people who have rejected what you are sharing will actually later apologize and thank you for being bold in sharing the truth. When I reflect on the number of people who have personally told me no, the number is easily in the thousands. While I would have preferred that everyone said yes, that is not how it works. The amazing works of God that I have seen through those that were open is well worth all the rejection that I have had to work through. Just like working out, there is pain, stress, and soreness as we get in shape. As you make a lifestyle out of praying for people and sharing the Gospel, you will build the mental toughness required to manage the rejection. Far greater than the satisfaction that comes from getting in shape is the joy that comes from seeing God change the lives of the people that cross your path!

12

Overcoming Apathy

LET'S FACE it, life is very busy. But God wants us to be available despite how we feel. The adversities we face and our response to them can serve as major stumbling blocks to seeing God move in powerful ways in our lives and in the lives of others. There is nothing wrong with having feelings of apathy, exhaustion, sadness, and a multitude of other emotions. This is common to us all. The reason I call them out is there is a daily temptation to let our feelings at any given moment govern how we respond to God and engage others.

As I reflect on how often I feel like doing ministry or being used by God, the majority of the time I don't feel like it. More commonly, I feel like not doing it at all. That is why I appreciate Paul's letter to the Romans and how he struggled with this challenge as well.

For what I am doing, I do not understand. For what I will to do, that I do not practice; but what I hate, that I do. If, then, I do what I will not to do, I agree with the law that it is good. But now, it is no longer I who do it, but sin that dwells in me. For I know that in me (that is, in my flesh) nothing good dwells; for to will is present with me, but how to perform what is good I do not find.

—Romans 7:15–18

Jesus also dealt with these very issues, as He was tempted in all ways and never sinned. As His followers, we must be aware that we will face these issues and need to *commit to push through these feelings* to make a difference in the life of others, to walk in power, and to see transformation in our walk with God.

Patience in tribulation and pushing through the desires of our flesh is much easier to *talk about* than it is to do. I am reminded of a trip I took that tested me tremendously in this area. One week I was on a multi-city trip for meetings, and I found myself flying out of Santa Barbara, California, to Denver, Colorado. The departing flight was over its weight limit and delayed. Since the flight was overbooked and late, the airline offered an unusually generous voucher and an upgrade if anyone was willing to take the next flight, which was scheduled to leave in four hours. It had already been a very long day for me, and I didn't want to do it, but the party I was traveling with all decided to take the offer, so I obliged, as well.

The expected four-hour wait turned into a seven-hour wait as the next flight was also late. When I finally got to the hotel, I learned that *they* were overbooked and could not honor the reservation I had made. I sat in the lobby for over an hour while the staff figured out another hotel that had capacity. The shuttle took what seemed like forever to come and even longer to get to the hotel where I would finally stay. When I opened the door to my room, it was just after 3:30 a.m.—and just as I was getting ready for bed, I felt God tell me He wanted me to run at 5:30 a.m.—after only two hours of sleep!

That was not what I wanted to hear in that moment, and it did not make me happy. Didn't God understand that I would have less than two hours to sleep and that I had a full day of meetings to be present for? To say that I did not want to do this would be a massive understatement. This was a test of my faith in the midst of being totally exhausted, but I have come to know that God is not limited by how I feel. God calls us to act because He has something planned, and I didn't want to miss it.

The hour and forty-five minutes of sleep flew by, the alarm went off, and I laced up my running shoes and headed for the lobby. I sure didn't feel like it, but nonetheless I persevered to run following the direction that God had given me. As I turned left onto the street, I came across another jogger—whom I had the sense that God wanted me to engage. I called out to the jogger, but she did not hear me. I felt God nudge me again, so I picked up my pace to see if she needed prayer. The woman accepted prayer for her life while we ran. This was a big test for me because she ran at a much faster pace than I did, and she did not stop for the prayer. I dug deep to keep up with her pace and prayed for her while we ran. She was thankful for the prayer, and I inquired if she had a relationship with Jesus. The woman did not have a relationship with Jesus, so I went on to share my testimony and the Gospel as we ran at a blistering pace. When I gave her an invitation to accept Christ, she accepted and then stopped to pray with me to give her heart to Jesus. I was so thankful to catch my breath and share that eternity-shaping moment on the street corner. There were many other ordained encounters that happened that morning—all glory to God! He is so faithful in that He provided tremendous grace to me to stay strong all day for all my meetings and a dinner event, even though I was operating on fumes.

Another obstacle can include the challenges that life tends to throw at us when we want to be available for God. One morning I was getting ready to go on a run, and I flushed the toilet. Water pooled at the bottom of the toilet and then began to flow across the bathroom floor. That is not how a toilet is supposed to work! I faced a crossroads in that moment. Did I put off my "run for God" and fix the toilet, or would I put His Kingdom first and trust that He would help me work it out later? I made the decision in that moment to continue with my plan for ministry, so I turned off the water to the toilet and laced up my running shoes.

The morning was filled with multiple encounters that would not have happened if I had let the plumbing issue dictate the day. As I ran that morning, I felt impressed to go up on the train platform, which was weird because it was closed. As I went up anyway, I could see a man in a car that I could not see from below, so I made my way over to his vehicle. It turned out that he accepted prayer for his situation as he was grieving the loss of a girlfriend. The Holy Spirit brought great comfort and peace in that time of prayer, and the man was very thankful. Next, I prayed for a city worker for safety as he painted the street, a student for grace on final exams, and a man and a woman at a bus stop for their lives. Another woman accepted prayer at the bus stop, and she marveled at the moving of the Holy Spirit in the prayer. When I asked if she had a relationship with Jesus, she said she did not. I shared my testimony and the Gospel, and she prayed with me to accept Jesus as her Savior. As she said "amen" at the end of the prayer, her bus stopped, the bus doors opened, and she stepped on to go to work. The perfect timing of God never ceases to amaze me! There were many other encounters that happened that morning because I didn't let the flooding toilet derail me from His plan. There are times in our lives when we need perspective from the Father, and He put this Scripture on my heart for that very purpose:

> *For consider Him who endured such hostility from sinners against Himself, lest you become weary and discouraged in your souls. You have not yet resisted to bloodshed, striving against sin.*
>
> —Hebrews 12:3–4

Overcoming Apathy

The struggles of life can be all-consuming and can cause us to be apathetic to what God asks us to do. There was a particular area of life that I was believing for breakthrough in, and I just seemed to encounter closed door after closed door, which had been very frustrating. Some obstacles we can navigate around, and others God wants us to go *through*. I have and will continue to trust Him that He will work all things together for my good even in the long, hot, seemingly unjust battles. Even though we face battles that are tough, God has prepared good works for us to walk in. I went to the gym, but the pool was closed on this particular Friday. I felt like I was supposed to go to the Jacuzzi (instead of leaving for a gym with a working pool, which would have been my norm). There was a woman there for whom I offered to pray. She declined, explaining that she prayed to her goddess; then she offered to cast a spell on me! Of course, I declined. She went on to share half truths about the merits of a pagan religion for the next fifteen minutes. I left her with the thought that Jesus is real, that He loved her more than she could possibly understand, that He wanted a relationship with her, and that she should seek out the truth in the matter. God loved this woman and was pursuing a relationship with her. That experience was unique, but it is like the work of planting, watering, and harvesting. Even when we are available for God to use in the midst of trials, we will still face rejection and resistance. Regardless of what the results of our availability may look like, it is critical that we stay on mission for Him.

There are times when God will call us into action when we don't feel like it and when conditions may be less than optimal. I remember a particular trip I was preparing for when the Paradise fires were raging in northern California. As my wife and I were talking, she made the comment, "Tell me you are not planning to go for any runs on this trip." She made this comment because the air quality was hazardous due to the fires, and she was concerned about my well-being. The thought immediately came to mind that people were going to hell and that we must share the Gospel. I shared this with her, and she just gave me one of "those looks." My wife is an amazing woman, and she has been extremely supportive of me. I put weight on her wisdom and concern, but God must have the final word.

The next morning, I felt God tell me to "go to the preacher." When God spoke this to my heart, I knew exactly what He was talking about. On a previous trip, I had prayed for a preacher who drove a utility truck. I remembered the parking lot where I had met the man, so I ran to that location. When I arrived where he had been parked the last time, he was not there. Since I was there, I had the thought to run around the area to see who else God might want to reach that day. I saw a security vehicle patrolling the area, so I ran over to the car to see if they needed prayer for anything. The security guard rolled down his window, and I offered to pray for him. The man went on to share amazing testimonies of how God had saved his life on multiple occasions. The man shared how he had been shot eight times in the last thirteen years; in the most recent incident, he had been shot by a 7.62-caliber round that nearly took his arm off. I prayed for the man and his life, and the Holy Spirit moved mightily. The man was blessed and marveled at the encounter. Next, I prayed for three different people that morning while heading to work. After that encounter, I prayed for a man waiting to start a new job, and the Holy Spirit brought him great peace, with him afterward making the comment about how hard things had been for him recently. I asked him if he had a relationship with Jesus, and he did not, so I shared my testimony, including the Gospel, then gave him the invitation to accept Christ. That man prayed with me to accept Jesus as his Savior right in front of a commercial job site.

As I continued on my run, I came across a man who was fixing a truck in the parking lot. I offered to pray for the man, and he asked for prayer for his autistic brother. After that prayer concluded, God prompted me about the preacher again, so I ran back to where he had been parked during our first encounter, and he was there. We had a great conversation, both of us sharing testimonies about God moving in our lives. He invited me to preach at his church in two weeks' time. I told him what was burning in my heart, and he said that was exactly what he wanted me to share with the congregation. (I would end up sharing at his church one evening when I was back in the area.) After concluding that conversation, I continued on my run and prayed for a man who requested prayer for some friends who'd been affected by the fires. I prayed for another man who was driving a big-rig for the Paradise fires. Then I came upon another semi-truck driver and offered to pray for him. The man accepted prayer for his friend's mother, who had been diagnosed with cancer. The man confirmed feeling the Holy Spirit move in the prayer. I asked him if he had a relationship with Jesus and he did not, so I shared my testimony, including the Gospel, and gave that truck driver an invitation to accept Christ. This large, stoic truck driver prayed with me to accept Jesus as his Savior as a tear rolled down his cheek. The best way to describe these moments is just *holy* as God's presence becomes tender on our hearts.

On this morning with terrible air quality, God had prepared so many rich divine encounters to bring hope and encouragement and demonstrate His radical love for so many people who were struggling with the wildfires as well as real problems in their lives. The eternity of those two men who encountered Jesus that morning was well worth what was required of me. The conditions that morning were very unusual. I would consider them an exception, and not the rule, but they illustrate an important point: Whether we face rain, wind, or even the most common opposition—not feeling like doing what the Lord is asking of us, we must push through the obstacles we encounter. We can be assured that if God is asking us to do something, there is purpose in it, and it is important that we listen and obey regardless of whether we feel like it or not.

13

No Time

ANOTHER OBSTACLE to overcome is, "Do I have enough time to help shape eternity?" One of the obstacles that can come up is how much time we perceive to have. We have so many demands on our time, including work, spouse, kids, extended family, sports, recreation, household responsibilities—and the list goes on. Our lives tend to be so full we can't even get to everything on our list, let alone become more available to be used by God. This is an area in which we need to seek God for wisdom and how He wants to use us. God has blessed us with time, talent, and treasure. It is important that we are intentional about how we steward these gifts in a way that honors Him.

One trap we need to be aware of is thinking that once our schedules are freed up, we will be more available for God. The truth is that this day will never come! Every season of our lives brings with it more than enough activities, hobbies, and challenges to consume all our attention and resources. When we are in college, we pour ourselves into going to class, studying, working a part-time job, spending time with friends, and having some fun along the way. When we start our careers, we throw ourselves fully into learning the industry and getting established. When we are married, we must learn how to do life together, balancing work, time together, and running a combined household. When kids enter the mix, we are learning how to parent and juggling school, activities, sports, music lessons, playdates, and the list goes on. Other phases of life bring a corresponding list of activities and responsibilities that can consume all our available resources. This life is like a vapor. We must number our days and put first things first.

Each of these roles is important and is certainly a part of what God has called us to do. . . I have learned that God specializes in using us in each of these capacities to co-labor with Him as He shapes eternity. I didn't think I had time either. I have a tendency to be very mission-oriented and linear in my thinking. My mission when I go to the grocery store is to buy groceries and then return home. My mission when I travel for meetings is to prepare for the meeting, travel to the location, conduct the meeting, and then return home after the meeting. What I have learned is that God has actually planned good works for me to walk in *while* I do these things. They don't happen every time, or even most of the time. God understands we have a schedule to keep to and responsibilities to take care of. That is why it is important for us to live intentionally, asking God if He has anyone whom He wants us to touch. It's a "boots on the ground," "on point" attitude.

Rarely does a walk with God require clearing our calendars, quitting our jobs, or taking some other major life-altering action. There are times when He will call us to do such things, in order to pull us out of a destructive lifestyle or into something new for Him. When we are called to take such a bold course of action, it is important that we seek God on the move, including the timing, and talk with godly people in our lives to be sure we are making wise decisions.

For most of us, though, God is looking to use us in normal ways, on a daily basis, with activities that are woven into our current calendar. Your

No Time

next encounter could be waiting for you on your next trip to the grocery store. You could be in a line at the grocery store just waiting for your turn to check out, and God may have a divine appointment in mind with the person waiting in front of you or behind you—a simple interaction that would take no more time than if you weren't being used by Him at all. But that interaction could make an eternal difference in the life of someone else, their family today, and even generations into the future. Jesus did remarkable things in the lives of countless people. How long does it take to be intentional? Just a few minutes. While the interactions are short in duration, their effect can be eternal. Jesus clearly told us that for those who believe, the works He did and greater we will do, as well.

This topic reminds me of a bike ride I once took. One of the ways I get exercise is by riding a twenty-three-mile loop near the river, by the waterfront, and through the city. On one particular day, I was about nine miles into my ride when my tire split, resulting in a flat tire. There was nothing I could do at that moment to repair the tire, so I called my wife, and luckily she was available to pick me up. The flat had occurred near the Aquarium of the Pacific, so there were tons of people coming and going. I had not planned for the flat tire. But I also knew that the flat tire did not catch God by surprise, and I wondered if He had anything planned while I waited for my wife to pick me up.

As I scanned the crowd, I asked God if there was anyone there whom He wanted me to talk to. There was a woman sitting stoically at a bus stop by herself, and I had the sense I was supposed to talk to her. I wheeled my bike over to her, let her know that God had put her on my heart, and asked if she needed prayer for anything. The woman immediately went from being very calm to weeping openly. She went on to explain, through many tears and deep sobs, how sad and anxious she had been. She had just had to get out of the house to try to clear her head. I prayed over this young woman in the midst of so much going on around us. God took the petition into a number of areas that we did not discuss, but the woman marveled as they were spot-on with what she was going through. Afterward, she asked if she could give me a hug, and I warned her that I was sweaty and smelled bad. Undeterred, she gave me a hug. Then I asked if she had a relationship with Jesus, and she did not. I shared my testimony, including the Gospel, and I gave her an invitation to accept Christ. Just as my wife pulled up, that young woman prayed to accept Jesus as her personal Lord and Savior.

When I reflect on this encounter, I can see the fingerprints of God all over it. It is important to note that going into the conversation, the outcome was not at all clear to me. There were literally dozens and dozens of people doing a variety of things there at that time. Cars were coming and going. I was frustrated about my flat tire and how I was going to fix it. The question of how long it was going to take for my wife to pick me up was swirling in my mind. With all the commotion and activity swirling around me, however, I still decided to be intentional and ask God if He had anyone He wanted me to talk to. I asked the question and *expected* God to answer. I asked the question and waited. When the answer came, it was not through an audible voice or a distinct vision, although God will use those as well. This message was a very subtle sense that I should talk to this lady who was sitting by herself at the bus stop, with nothing to go on other than a very subtle impression. What was required next was faith on my part. I needed to step out. I needed to embrace the awkwardness of the moment. I had to accept the very real possibility that she would not be interested in anything I had to say. I had to be willing to be potentially rejected and feel silly. *In light of all that Jesus suffered in order to set people free, the risk of rejection was tiny and well worth it, so I stepped out in faith.* And through my simple availability, God did a beautiful and eternity-shaping work in the heart of that woman.

No Time

We entered this life with nothing, and when our earthly life is over, we will take no material possessions with us. What matters most is having a relationship with Jesus and how we steward what He has trusted us with in our time, talent, treasure, and relationships. One way of being intentional about how we steward our time for Him is through structured and unstructured means. Unstructured means are those opportunities that present themselves during the course of our day-to-day lives. The structured investment of time is scheduled time for Kingdom-related work.

This structured time could involve volunteering at the church ushering, working with kids, going on mission trips, working in the parking lot, leading worship, leading a small group, or a variety of other ministry pursuits. If you are not already involved, I would highly encourage you to start. Think about an area in your church you are drawn to or have a gift for. Even if it is just a few hours per month, I would encourage you to get started. There is something life changing that happens when we put the teaching we receive on Sunday into action. Our relationship with God grows in beautiful ways, and our understanding of Scripture takes on new meaning when we are active for God.

14

Not Knowing What to Say

ANOTHER OBSTACLE we face can either give us second thoughts or prevent us from sharing the Gospel. That is *being concerned about not knowing what to say when we talk to people about Jesus.* Because people can respond in a variety of ways and have a multitude of questions, there is the very real possibility that something will come up that we will not know how to answer—if we rely solely on what we know or have had experience with on our own. A person may have beliefs that we don't understand or hold an adamant position we may think we are not equipped to address. Just as in all areas of our call to follow Jesus, God has equipped us with power, wisdom, and boldness to address this concern, as well. Jesus assures us that we will have the words we will need through the Holy Spirit. The part that can be difficult to grasp and is counter to our culture is that we may not know in advance. The following verse assures us that even in those circumstances, God will absolutely provide what is needed in that conversation.

> "Now when they bring you to the synagogues and magistrates and authorities, do not worry about how or what you should answer, or

what you should say. For the Holy Spirit will teach you in that very hour what you ought to say."

—Luke 12:11–12 NKJV

These beautiful verses in Luke share what Jesus' disciples were to do when they encountered the priests, magistrates, and spiritual authorities of their day. These were learned men, those in positions of religious power at that time. If there was ever a group of people who could be difficult to reason with, this would be them. Today, this instruction of Jesus still applies. The name of Jesus is above every name. All true wisdom flows from the Father. God knows what these people are thinking, how they reason, and any lies the enemy has planted in their hearts that would keep them away from the redeeming truth of a relationship with Jesus. God knows the beginning from the end, and there is nothing that will ever catch Him by surprise. This includes our interactions with others as we represent Him.

Then Jesus said to them, "When you lift up the Son of Man, then you will know that I am He, and that I do nothing of Myself; but as My Father taught Me, I speak these things."

—John 8:28 NKJV

Jesus gave us the example we should follow. He relied on the Father to teach Him what He should say. Jesus had an unshakable confidence that the Father would thoroughly equip Him for everything He was asked to do, both in deed and in the words He spoke, including if He was witnessing to a clever lawyer, a crafty scribe, or a cunning Pharisee. The Father gave Jesus wisdom for every encounter to fulfill what He had asked Jesus to do. The Scripture gives us an example both in how the conversations went and how effective the wisdom of God was in every situation.

> *"Do you not believe that I am in the Father, and the Father in Me? The words that I speak to you I do not speak on My own authority; but the Father who dwells in Me does the works. Believe Me that I am in the Father and the Father in Me, or else believe Me for the sake of the works themselves."*
>
> —John 14:10–11 NKJV

Jesus gives us further insight that as He was obedient to what God asked Him to do, the Father, who dwelt in Him, did the works. This is a good reminder that our role is simply to maintain our obedience, availability, and faith. Just as Jesus trusted in the Father, we must follow His example and do the same. God's ways are above our ways, and His thoughts are above our thoughts. God's Word does not return void, but it accomplishes that which He sends it to do (Isaiah 55:11). When we do as He has asked of us, we can trust that He will work through us to do what needs to be done in every encounter.

Each encounter that I have is unique. One of the ways God directs what I say is how He inspires my thoughts when I am reaching people for Him. The way this happens for me is not that I am being told to say things in a particular order, but *I trust what God brings to my mind in the moment.* An example of this once took place when I was checking into a hotel and was talking to the manager on duty. In the course of our conversation, I shared that I often pray for people and see God do wonderful things in their lives. The man said he was an atheist, and then he shared how he had been told he was going to go to hell. He emphatically shared that he was not the "church type." But people had told him that because of his tattoos, his rings, and his alternative lifestyle, there was nothing he could do to avoid going to hell. I told that man that what those people said was not true. Jesus died on the cross so he could be forgiven. I shared many testimonies with him specifically concerning the healing of people who had had gods other than Jesus. I shared the testimony of the Buddhist woman at my gym whom God had healed of a sleeping disorder, and that touched this man deeply. Another testimony came to mind that I shared, of another woman whom I had prayed for—she had major issues of fear and anxiety, but she reported feeling "something lift off of her" as I prayed. Much to my surprise, this man went on to share how he only slept a few hours at a time; that he had issues with fear and anxiety; and that he'd just gotten back from a rehab refresher. God had given me the exact testimonies that applied to what he was contending with. He accepted prayer, then told me he experienced feeling a "tingly sensation" as I spoke the love, acceptance and promises of Jesus over him. I encouraged him to be open as God continued to seek him out, and the man said he would. *This encounter was a great example to me that I don't need to have it all figured out in advance, or even have precise instructions to go on, before I share the Gospel and offer to pray for people.* Over and over, as I step out in faith for God, He brings to mind the testimonies I should share, then anoints them and guides the conversation where it needs to go.

Another way God helps us is by giving us favor with the people we talk to. God holds the hearts of men in His hand, and the Holy Spirit will create an openness for the conversations He wants us to have. One day as I was eating lunch, a couple sat next to me, and I felt like I was supposed to talk to them. This encounter really stretched me, as the man was huge—very well-built, with a full sleeve of tattoos on both arms and a presence that would make anyone with bad intentions seriously reconsider their course of action. Yet I pushed through my discomfort, politely interrupted their conversation, and asked them if they needed prayer for anything. It turned out that they were believers and the nicest couple. They were so excited that I would offer to pray for them. The couple was getting married in six months, and she needed a new job and was facing serious fear. He was a corrections officer at the prison. We prayed together, and they were so thankful. This was another important reminder not to judge a book by its cover and that God has equipped us with everything we will need to do what He asks of us.

The people around us will often give us the impression that everything is okay, and if we only were to go by their appearance, we might never approach them. This next example occurred in a hotel gym while I was traveling. A young, well-built man in the gym had a confident presence, and this particular situation, I did not have an impression or any indication to engage with him, but I figured I was running on the treadmill anyway. I would just see if there was anything that might present an opener for conversation. I struck up a conversation with him that made its way to talking about God and how awesome He is. As we talked, a number of testimonies came to mind involving fear, anxiety, and deliverance, and I shared them with this young man. These were total "God thoughts," as nothing about this man's appearance or countenance would give any indication that he was struggling in these areas. But the man totally surprised me by telling me that I was talking right to him, as he had recently been crushed by fear, frustration, and uncertainty. He accepted prayer, and the Holy Spirit impacted him in that prayer. The man was so thankful! It was another important reminder of how limited I am in what I observe, and that God is so faithful in providing all that is needed in every interaction.

God works through us as we follow Him, giving us wisdom in how to conduct our conversations even when initially a person may have no interest in God or prayer. One night as I was walking to dinner, I passed a man sitting on a bench who stood out to me. I approached the man and told him that God had put him on my heart, then I inquired if he needed prayer for anything. The man was quick to reject my offer and told me that he "was not into that." I responded with kindness, telling him how much God loved him, about the countless good thoughts He had toward the man along with the great plan He had for his life. As I spoke the promises of God over him, God moved on his heart, and tears filled the man's eyes. Even though I had not yet started praying, the Holy Spirit was quickly moving in the conversation. I went on to share testimonies of answered prayer with him, along with my own testimony and the Gospel. His attitude totally changed, and he prayed with me to receive Jesus as his Savior right there on that bench! Even though there was initial rejection in the conversation, the Holy Spirit moved powerfully in his heart, inspired me to share the right testimonies, and prepared the man to receive Jesus. God knew exactly what was needed, and He used my simple availability to woo this man's heart with His love. When we understand that God is actively drawing people into a relationship with Himself, it is very liberating, because we can simply rely on His sufficiency in the moment and not get bogged down with trying to figure out what to say.

There are times when God will also give us discernment related to what people say. If we rely only on our human understanding, we can draw the wrong conclusions. One day I was taking an Uber back from the airport, and I struck up a conversation with my driver that soon made its way to God. I started sharing testimonies of how God had been doing beautiful things in people's lives. The man shared that he prayed to God, but as he spoke, it became apparent to me, in my spirit, that he was just doing this in a general sense; he did not have a personal relationship with Jesus. The only way I can describe this insight is that it was simply inspired by the Holy Spirit. I shared my testimony, including the Gospel, and gave him an invitation to accept Christ. He accepted my invitation and prayed with me to receive Jesus as his Savior as we drove in that Uber to my house. He told me he felt very good after accepting Jesus; he even felt like he was going to cry. I told him that it was about to get more intense, then I prayed the love, heart, plans, and promise of God over his life. The man was wearing sunglasses so I could not see his eyes directly, but the Holy

Spirit moved powerfully in that prayer and soon I saw tears streaming out from under his sunglasses as God moved on his heart as only He can do. I always enjoy seeing the goodness of God absolutely overwhelm someone with tears of joy! Here was this large, distinguished African American man with tears streaming down his cheeks as he encountered the love of Jesus and hope filled his heart. It was wonderful!

God does something beautiful and personal in every encounter. He inspires each conversation, and the Holy Spirit moves to bring hope, healing, and breakthrough. As we become more available for God, we will gain a greater appreciation for how He works. This will build our confidence that He will bring the right words to us each and every time. God never changes; He is the same yesterday, today, and forever. The work He did through the ministry of Jesus and the apostles, He desires to do through us. Just as Jesus trusted that God would give Him the right words to speak, we must do the same. Our walk with God and our availability to Him teaches us how to let Him work through us; the key ingredient is faith. We must trust Him. *Faith* is an action word—a verb. Faith requires us to be obedient and step out of the boat. Peter did not know he would be able to walk on water until he stepped out of the boat. If you are concerned about having the right things to say, the greatest remedy is your experience of the faithfulness of God *when you take a risk*. It may feel awkward to offer to pray for someone, especially a stranger. It feels risky when you step out and share your faith. *But by faith, God will teach you in the very moment what you need to say.* As we see God move through our availability, it will inspire us to want to be used more often, and encounter after encounter, we will see the greater things that Jesus promised.

15

God's Fingerprints

AS WE become more active and available for God to reach others, we will also develop a greater awareness of His expressions of radical love in our own lives. God knows us better than we know ourselves. Not only does He prepare good works for us to walk in, but He blesses us with countless kindnesses, mercies, and gifts to help us throughout our lives. We must be diligent in observing and remembering them. This is essential for living a fruitful and productive life with an ongoing sense of gratitude toward Him. This perspective will help us through our own battles and serve as a powerful testimony to encourage others in their own trials.

One of the ministries in which I serve is the Helps Ministry at Cottonwood Church. We help single moms, the elderly, the disabled, and those in a financial bind with repairs and construction projects at their homes. This ministry serves those in our congregation and our community with yard work, electrical, flooring, drywall, plumbing, and other types of needs. The entire team is made up of volunteers. When we start our projects, I gather the team and the family we are helping together for a prayer. I pray that God would help us to work together, that we would have grace for the job, that there would be safety for the team and excellence in what we are doing, and that as we worked the family would be reminded of how much God loved them and that He cared not only for the big things in their lives, but the details too.

One morning my water heater went out, and I purchased a new water heater to install. Since I had not done it before, I called a friend who worked with me in the ministry to see if he knew anyone who could help me with the project. He said yes, that he could help me, and he came over to my house. My friend looked at the situation and determined that the old water heater did not need to be replaced, but it simply needed a new thermocouple, which ended up costing less than twenty dollars. He replaced the thermocouple and saved me over $750 dollars in a new water heater and parts! That old water heater lasted over ten more years, even though it was very old at the time of the repair.

My friend then asked me if I had any slow drains at that time, because he had his drain-clearing snake on his truck. What my friend did not know was that my bathtub had not been draining properly for over a year. My boys were very young at the time, and we used that tub daily. We were very busy, and a slow bathtub drain had never made it to the top of my priority list to address. While he was in the bathroom clearing that drain, I was in the kitchen heating up some coffee, and the Holy Spirit dropped on me very powerfully. God spoke clearly to my heart that He cares about the details of *my* life too. I teared up realizing that the God of the universe cared about me and my slow bathtub drain. Even though this took place well over ten years ago, I can still vividly remember it, and it serves as one of many reminders of God's beautiful attention to our lives. God worked through the skills and availability of my friend to reach me in a practical and powerful way.

When He had stopped speaking, He said to Simon, "Launch out into the deep and let down your nets for a catch." But Simon answered and said to Him, "Master, we have toiled all night and caught nothing; nevertheless at Your word I will let down the net." And when they had done this, they caught a great number of fish, and their net was breaking.

—Luke 5:4–6

This Scripture means a tremendous amount to me as it serves as a great example of how Jesus worked two thousand years ago and how He is working in our lives today. My wife has the gift of hospitality. She loves to entertain and cook for people, whether it is baking something special for the Bible study group that meets at our house or hosting a carb dinner for the high school water polo team. Her kitchen is one of the places where God works through her to touch the lives of others. The kitchen sink we had was very old, and it required regular bleaching to maintain a clean look as the protective coating had worn off. Over time, the faucet began to leak and needed to be replaced.

For the replacement of the kitchen sink, Michelle had a very specific style in mind that was not readily available. She had been looking for a white, cast-iron sink with a deep single-tub configuration. The problem was that Kohler only made a few different varieties of this style of sink, and only one was stocked locally. I bought the one sink I could find that would come close to this configuration. But when we removed the old sink and tried to put in the new one, the sink did not fit properly because of how the original hole had been cut in the granite. Now we had a problem, as we had destroyed the other faucet and the old sink was out and in really bad shape.

To make matters worse, I called Kohler to find out the lead time on ordering a custom sink directly, only to find out one of their factories had burned down and we were looking at a minimum of six months to get a new sink from them. I went to my local Home Depot, the local Lowe's, and all the other kitchen appliance/sink distributers nearby, and no one had a sink that met the requirements. The whole process was extremely frustrating, and I didn't know what to do.

Just like Jesus instructed Simon to cast his nets again, God put on my heart to go to a different Lowe's and take a look. My natural reaction was to ignore this thought, as I had already been to multiple Lowe's stores, and the inventory had been the same at each one. Nevertheless, I did as God asked and went to the store He put on my heart. To my wild surprise, the store had the one Kohler sink that would properly fit the hole—and it was white, with the proper basin depth, hole configuration, and tub layout! The sink was in perfect condition and marked down over 80 percent. I would have paid list price plus just to get the sink, but God not only had it available for me, but He had it at a massive discount because He knew that Michelle needed a sink and that I love a good deal! God is amazing!

God's fingerprints are numerous and can be found across our lives. While we aim to make good choices and do the right thing, we inevitably make mistakes and bad decisions. There are times when God needs to correct us, and those times are never pleasant. One of the beautiful aspects of our walk with God is how He restores us on the other side of a correction. Jesus gives us an example of this when He told Peter, before He was crucified, that Peter would deny Jesus three times. Peter was insistent that he would never deny Jesus, but it came to pass exactly as Jesus had prophesied, and Peter denied Jesus three times. Even though Peter had left the ministry, Jesus did not give up on Peter, and the Scripture below tells the story of how Jesus restored Peter and called him back into the ministry:

> *So when they had eaten breakfast, Jesus said to Simon Peter, "Simon, son of Jonah, do you love Me more than these?" He said to Him, "Yes, Lord; You know that I love You." He said to him, "Feed My lambs."*

> *He said to him again a second time, "Simon, son of Jonah, do you love Me?" He said to Him, "Yes, Lord; You know that I love You." He said to him, "Tend My sheep." He said to him the third time, "Simon, son of Jonah, do you love Me?" Peter was grieved because He said to him the third time, "Do you love Me?" And he said to Him, "Lord, You know all things; You know that I love You." Jesus said to him, "Feed My sheep."*
>
> —John 21:15–17

God is the same yesterday, today, and forever. The Bible can be trusted, and it gives us a blueprint of how God works. The difference is that God works through you and me to restore others, even if we don't have the backstory. For God to effectively work through us, it is important that we are available and that we do what God asks of us. Here is a story of how God restored me after correcting me.

I accepted Jesus as my Lord and Savior in 1995. Some people have radical conversion testimonies, followed by being used by God very quickly. That is not my story. God wanted to work through me, but I did not cooperate with Him. When God would put it on my heart to do something or get involved with a particular ministry, I would make excuses or ignore the conviction until it went away. This tug-of-war went on for over ten years, even though I was attending church regularly. The desire to read the Bible began to grow in me, so I started spending more time in the Word. One day I was reading in the book of Acts, and I came across this verse:

> *And the evil spirit answered and said, "Jesus I know, and Paul I know; but who are you?"*
>
> —Acts 19:15

The backstory on this verse is that unusual miracles were being done by Paul and the early Church. Casting out evil spirits was one of the miracles that were being performed. In this particular Scripture, the seven sons of Sceva, a Jewish chief priest, were attempting to cast out an evil spirit, even though they were not followers of Jesus. The spirit responded by challenging their authority and sent them away naked and afraid. There are times when we read Scripture and God anoints the written Word to carry power and a specific purpose. This is also referred to as a *"rhema word"* from God. When I read this Scripture, it absolutely came alive and spoke to my heart. God brought a deep and unpleasant conviction to me about how I was not listening to Him and not being available for the plans He had for me.

While it is difficult to fully describe the weight and power of that moment, it had a radical impact on my heart and my relationship with God. I repented for my disobedience and made a deal with God. My heart was that regardless of what He asked of me, I would be obedient and do what He said to do. If that meant digging a hole for four hours and then filling it back in again for four hours, I would do it. I can't say that I have shot 100 percent on obedience since that day, but my follow-through on what God has asked of me improved dramatically from that time on.

A number of years ago, I sent a friend a text about an encounter I'd had. The man I sent it to loves God who hears regularly from the Lord. God gave him something very specific that probably seemed strange to him, but he passed it on anyway. The text he sent me was this:

> There was a time when we were afraid of the devil, now he is afraid of you, Jesus I know, Paul I know and John I know.

When I looked back, I realized that twelve years after that corrective conviction, God spoke through a friend to restore me. This experience was deeply personal and very encouraging to me. It reminded me that the

God of the universe knows us personally, and that He knows all, from the beginning to the end. This experience reminds me that when God gives me a word or an impression, I should pass it on, even if I don't have context or understand its meaning. God knows and the person you are talking to will know. Obedience in these matters is important, as it could change the trajectory of their life or bring about closure to an important matter.

In this chapter, each of the testimonies that I shared with you were deeply impactful to me personally. Take some time to consider the times in your life when God has really helped you and it was deeply impactful to you personally. God uses both His simple kindnesses and the times when He has done the sensational to encourage us *and* those around us. We want to have an inventory of God's faithfulness to help us to have a heart of gratitude. Meditating on God's faithfulness in previous struggles helps us to navigate the tough times we are presently in and those that are to come. The other reason is that God will use His faithfulness in *our* lives to both encourage others and to build *their* faith for victory in *their* own struggles. Remembering how God has encouraged us will also help us when He gives a simple word, a conviction to do something, or encouragement to share with someone else. When we have testimonies ready and front of mind, we are equipped to help the people who will cross our paths.

16

Divine Protection

*He who dwells in the secret place of the Most High shall abide under the shadow of the Almighty. I will say of the L*ORD*, "He is my refuge and my fortress; my God, in Him I will trust." Surely He shall deliver you from the snare of the fowler and from the perilous pestilence. He shall cover you with His feathers, and under His wings you shall take refuge; His truth shall be your shield and buckler. You shall not be afraid of the terror by night, nor of the arrow that flies by day, nor of the pestilence that walks in darkness, nor of the destruction that lays waste at noonday.*

—Psalm 91:1–6

GOD IS so awesome in the protection He provides for us. Psalm 91 has been a foundational Scripture on which I have stood over the years. It has brought me great peace and encouragement, serving to remind me of the sufficiency of God's protection. One thing that will build and maintain our faith is when we recognize what God has done for us and others. As we do this, we will see our faith building, and it helps us to live a life of gratitude and contentment. God has been very faithful in protecting me and my family across the many roles that we have in life, whether it be our family life, our work, our ministry, or the times when we are out having fun. Building our faith regularly helps us to be equipped to be obedient when God asks us to reach the people around us, whom He loves so much.

God will use the testimonies of His goodness in our lives to also build faith in others. Here are a few stories of God's divine protection in my own life, both during my times of specific ministry and just in living life. My hope is that you will find them both encouraging and helpful in bringing stories to mind of times in your own life when God has done the same for you.

The first story relates to a time after I had accepted Christ and was in my first year of marriage. I started having abdominal pain that grew progressively worse. I went to several doctors, but no one could determine what was wrong with me. The pain got, to the point that it felt like I could feel my organs functioning and I would be doubled over on the floor of our apartment. This was a very scary experience, as I was totally miserable and no one could explain it. We finally went to one more doctor's appointment, and a physician's assistant actually recognized my condition. He had been a field medic in Vietnam and had seen a similar situation twice when he was over there. His diagnosis proved to be correct, and I was sent right in for surgery. I had a massive infection behind my belly button that was near bursting. What made it unusual is that I had retained a part of my navel that goes away in most people after they are born, but mine did not; instead, mine became infected. What are the chances that I would eventually see a PA who had seen such a rare condition *twice before in Vietnam*? Zero. God uses many vessels to protect and look after His people. That attentive PA was God's vessel for me, and he saved my life. If that infection had burst and gotten into my bloodstream, it would have certainly been fatal, but God had other plans for me.

Divine Protection

Another story that comes to mind is from a time when I was in Mexico with a friend. Where we were staying was about forty minutes from the airport via a high-speed toll road. Since the toll road didn't have a lot of people on it and it was a freeway, the speeds that folks would travel was pretty high. My friend drove me to the airport and dropped me off without incident. Later that day, my friend called to report that he had a slow leak in one of his tires, so he went to a tire store to get it checked out. When they looked at his tires, they identified a major problem: One of tires was extremely worn—but the spot was on the inside, so it could not be easily seen from the outside. This tire had a large spot that had worn through the tread *and* the steel belt—all that was keeping air in the tire was a very thin skin of rubber that you could easily push into with your finger. Given how hot it was and how fast we were driving, it is a total miracle that tire did not blow out on that high-speed toll road. God had totally saved us, and we had no idea at the time what He was doing!

Another example that comes to mind is from an encounter I had in my neighborhood. One morning I ran by a train station near my house. There was a handicapped woman in a wheelchair nearby. I ran over and told her that God had put her on my heart and asked if she would like prayer for anything. This woman wanted nothing to do with me or prayer at all, and she strongly declined. I didn't think much of it, and I just continued on my day. A few months later, I was at a stoplight in that vicinity waiting for a light to change, and the same woman in the wheelchair came rolling up right next to me. I didn't say anything to her and just waited for the light to change. When the light changed, I waited a moment before stepping into the crosswalk. As I was about to step into the intersection, I noticed motion out of the corner of my eye. Much to my horror, a van was racing up the arterial street, and it blew the fully red light without even slowing down. As I turned my head to see the van, my hand dropped down and stopped the woman in the wheelchair from going into the intersection.

Had I not stopped both myself and her, we would have absolutely been run down by that van that blazed by within inches of where we stood. The woman looked up at me and was extremely thankful. She called me her "guardian angel" and then gladly accepted prayer. The event that day completely changed our relationship. Even though I did not see her a lot, the handful of times I saw her after that crosswalk event always had her happy to see me, and we would marvel at God's divine protection that day. I became the "guardian angel" to the woman who wanted nothing to do with me when we first met!

Sometimes God helps us through unanswered prayer, and this next story is an example of this. A friend had invited me down to Mexico for some end-of-striped-marlin-season fishing. The first part of our adventure had us bringing the boat over from Mazatlán to Cabo San Lucas, about 180 miles. There was wind and rough seas as we made the crossing, but it wasn't terrible. The fishing that followed was much lighter than usual. The last time I had been down there, we'd caught and released over forty striped marlin. This time we caught and released a total of three. We prayed and believed throughout the trip that our fortunes would change, but they just did not. After I flew home, however, I got a call from my friend exclaiming how God had answered prayer. Given the amount of catching that went on, I was a little confused by the comment. My friend went on to explain that they had the boat taken out of the water for an insurance survey. When they took the boat out of the water, they discovered that one of the underwater lights had come off, leaving only a broken fixture backing, blocking a hole that was two inches in diameter. If that backing had come out, the boat could have sunk in just minutes as the bilge pump would not have been able to keep up with the inflow. The boat could have sunk coming across from Mazatlán, in the marina, or when we were out fishing. If we had caught more fish, the process of catching them would have almost certainly blown out that light backing, which would have caused the boat to sink! The reason for this is that when you catch a marlin, the boat captain backs the boat down on the fish, and that would have caused heavy, direct pressure on the failed fixture. We were so thankful for unanswered prayers on that trip!

The last example of God's protection occurred when I was traveling in the northern part of California. I was on an early morning run and was heading back to the hotel. I ran across a freeway overpass and came to a stop at a red light. The light changed, I stepped into the crosswalk and a car across the street began frantically honking. As I stopped to look at the car honking, a semi-truck blew through the red light and through the crosswalk, coming so close to me I could have reached out and touched it with my hand. Had I taken one more step, that truck would have run me down, and it is highly unlikely I would have survived. I ran over and thanked the woman who had just saved my life. I let her know that I see miracles regularly and inquired if she needed prayer for anything. She was struggling with heavy anxiety and depression. I prayed for that woman that morning, and the Holy Spirit moved, bringing peace, hope, and love as the woman wept. God is so good that He had planned a great exchange that morning. She saved my life, and I had the opportunity to pray for her, for breakthrough in her situation.

Take some time and consider God's faithfulness in your life, how He has either protected or provided for you. If you are having trouble remembering such times, ask God to draw your attention to these life experiences. Even though the Bible was written over two thousand years ago, God's Word is just as true and relevant today as it was back then. As we study Scripture and its application in our life, we grow in our relationship with God. This is true not only with what we are actively going through, but also in what God has helped us through. You will be surprised as you take time to see God's hand at work in your life. Then, God will put people in your life where that experience will help you to relate with them. Some encounters will be so specific that God could cross your path with someone who is literally in the middle of what you have already been delivered from. Those experiences will be so encouraging for the other person and for you. God gives us an example of how He does this in the book of Genesis through the life of Joseph:

> *"But as for you, you meant evil against me; but God meant it for good, in order to bring it about as it is this day, to save many people alive."*
> —Genesis 50:20

Even though the brothers of Joseph had evil plans for him, God delivered Joseph from their plans and used that difficult season to prepare Joseph for an incredible destiny. God used Joseph to redeem his family, save his people, and make a difference globally as he helped Pharaoh prepare for and navigate a seven-year famine that was to come. God is the same yesterday, today, and forever. God has used the story of Joseph in many encounters I have had to bring hope to those facing prison, in prison, and those who have come out of prison. Just as God has saved you, He has also prepared good works for you to walk in, and He has a plan to share your story to encourage others in their trial, to point people to Jesus, and to help Him to establish His Kingdom on earth as it is in heaven.

# 17

Love

Watch, stand fast in the faith, be brave, be strong. Let all that you do be done with love.

—1 Corinthians 16:13–14

THE ROAD less traveled is an adventure with God, without comparison, and is foundational to following Jesus. He set the example, but I would be doing you a disservice if I did not talk about the most important part. The most important part to being used mightily by God is that *we have His heart*. God sent Jesus to die on the cross for us because He *loved* us. Jesus left heaven to walk as a man, living a sinless life, dying a horrible death on the cross, and becoming sin for us, because He *loves* us. The motive for the ministry of Jesus Christ was *love*. We get to learn His love and live it. We get to love others with His love. The heart for powerful ministry and fruitful lives has always been, is, and will always be love. This must be our first and most powerful motivation. Jesus prioritizes the two most important commandments in the gospel of Mark:

> *Jesus answered him, "The first of all the commandments is: 'Hear, O Israel, the L*ord* our God, the L*ord* is one. And you shall love the L*ord*

> *your God with all your heart, with all your soul, with all your mind, and with all your strength.' This is the first commandment. And the second, like it, is this: 'You shall love your neighbor as yourself.' There is no other commandment greater than these."*
>
> —Mark 12:29–31

The powerful moves of the Holy Spirit that we see manifested in so many ways are an expression of God's love for the people we encounter. *Nearly every prayer I pray over people begins with a request that the person being prayed for would experience the authentic love of Jesus in a fresh, powerful, and deeply personal way.* I pray they would experience what is the height, depth, width, and length of that love and that they would be filled with the fullness of God. This is the will and the heart of God. When we pray the will and heart of God for people, God responds. God yearns that every person would have a deep and abiding relationship with Him. When we are available for Him to love other people through us, God responds in beautiful, powerful, and surprising ways. When we pray according to His will, God answers our prayers, transforming lives, healing bodies, mending broken hearts, breaking addiction, and drawing the people He loves so much into redemptive relationships with Him.

The greatest expression of God's love for us can be found in one of the most-quoted Scriptures found in the book of John:

> *"For God so loved the world that He gave His only begotten Son, that whoever believes in Him should not perish but have everlasting life."*
>
> —John 3:16

This is why the Great Commission is so important—because we have been given the role of sharing this truth with the people whom God loves so much. There are times when God will actually share this amazing truth with people through unusual means. This next story is an example of this.

One day I was walking through the shower area of the gym, and I saw a man getting ready to take a shower. The man had long hair and was of Indian descent. Thankfully, he was still dressed when God put him on my heart. Even though it was very awkward for me, I walked over and asked him if he needed prayer for anything. The man gave me a puzzled look and asked me what I meant. I told him that I pray to Jesus for people and I see God do miracles. At that point, the man recognized the name of Jesus and told me a story. He told me that he'd had a dream in which he was about to be nailed to the cross for his sins. The man shared how Jesus took his place on the cross. I asked him if he had ever prayed to receive Jesus as his Savior. The man told me that after everything Jesus had done for him, it was the least he could do. I prayed with that man to receive Jesus as his Savior right there in the shower area of the gym. Jesus is so amazing that He died on the cross for us, and He appears to people in dreams to let them know! If I had let the awkwardness of the moment stop me, I would have never had the opportunity to hear about this man's amazing experience with Jesus or share in that holy moment that God had ordained.

There will be days when the love of God will draw us into conversations with people whom He wants to heal and deliver, but they will not be open to it. One of the reasons we must not be deterred in these encounters is that God will use our interaction to draw them into relationship with Him even when it appears to be negative. God has other work planned for us, so we need to shake off the rejection in order to reach other people. One trip I took is an example of this. I was on a flight and sat next to a woman with whom I struck up a conversation that made its way to God and the amazing work He does in the lives of people. As we talked, I had the impression that God wanted to do something powerful for this woman in the area of identity and peace. The woman later shared how she struggled mightily with issues of fear and anxiety. I offered to pray for her but she was not open to prayer and just wanted to argue with me. This doesn't happen often, but it really grieved me as I knew that God wanted to set her free, but she just wasn't open to it at that time.

Later that night, I was heading to dinner at one of my favorite local restaurants, which was attached to a large mall in the area. As I waited to turn into the parking lot, I noticed a large, well-built African American man with a hand truck. I had the sense that I was to go over to him, but I didn't have anything more to go on other than the thought. I pulled into the parking lot, parked my car, and walked over to him. I told him that God had put him on my heart and I was curious if he needed prayer for anything. The man went on to share that he was a semi-pro football player who had just sprained his ankle in practice. He was very worried because if he could not perform, he was going to lose his contract. I prayed for him and asked Jesus to heal him. When the prayer concluded, I asked him to try out his ankle and move it to test it out. The man began to move his ankle up and down. He looked at his ankle, and then he looked at me. I asked him to tell me, on a scale of one to ten, what the pain level was. He said it was a six, but he had a very puzzled look on his face. He continued moving the ankle in circles, then put his full weight on the left ankle and started doing toe raises with his full body weight on the previously sprained ankle. The man was completely surprised and asked me who I was. I asked him if he had a relationship with Jesus, and the man said yes. I told him that Jesus had just healed him. Jesus loved that man. His career was important to God. The miraculous healing that took place in that parking lot was an expression of God's incredible love and sufficiency for that man.

As we are active in sharing the love of Jesus with people, we will have days when we will see God's love expressed in a multitude of ways. Most of the time, I would characterize God's communication with me to be through "subtle impressions," perhaps of a person standing out to me amidst others or a sense to go in a certain direction. There are days when

Love

His communication will be more specific. The following is an example of the variety of ways in which God encourages others and expresses His love to us.

There was a time when I was traveling to a particular city on a regular basis. Hotel rates had a tendency to fluctuate pretty dramatically, based on events that were taking place, which resulted in a fair amount of pricing variability. Since I am fairly flexible on location, I would choose accommodations based on the most competitive rate, which had me staying in various locations but often in an unpredictable fashion. As God would have it, I ended up staying in one particular hotel from time to time. At this particular hotel, there was a night manager whom I would pray for whenever I would see him. The man shared how he was atheist who lived an alternate lifestyle, and he had been told throughout his life that he could never go to heaven because of his tattoos and the life he had lived. God opened a door for a relationship with this man. Every time I would be in town, he was working, and he was inevitably in the midst of some kind of turmoil. This would open the door for prayer, and he would experience the power of the Holy Spirit. I shared the Gospel with him during our initial conversation, but he was not ready yet to accept the Lord. After each successive encounter, I would ask him if he was ready to accept Christ. Over time, the man would give me a percentage of how close he was. God's love is both powerful and persistent!

On this particular trip, I saw this particular night manager and inquired how he was doing. The man shared that his niece was having some serious health challenges, but the doctors could not figure out what was wrong with her. We prayed together that God would heal her. God uses a variety of ways to heal. There are times when He will heal in a moment. Other times He will bring healing over time. God also uses doctors to bring discovery and healing as well. The following morning, the manager and I were talking, and he shared a praise report. The doctors had found a highly unusual condition in his niece—she had a twisted tube that was inhibiting her ability to digest the necessary medication. The discovery was both miraculous and a huge encouragement to the family. I asked the man if he was finally ready to accept Jesus that day, and he smiled, then told me he was 96 percent of the way there.

After our conversation, I headed out for my morning run. I prayed for my bus driver, who confirmed feeling the Holy Spirit and thanked me, saying he really needed it. I prayed for a security guard, and she was thankful. I prayed for two different truck drivers and a man driving a Cadillac, all of whom confirmed feeling the Holy Spirit. I prayed for a man driving a semi-truck and a group of four men in a homeless camp. As I ran over a bridge, the Holy Spirit dropped the question into my heart: *Is it possible to walk with Me and not be changed?* I just wept at the presence of the Holy Spirit and the goodness of God. While I see the Holy Spirit moving in the people for whom I pray, rarely do I experience it myself, which is what made this expression of God's love so special to me.

On my flight home later that day, my left arm began to hurt in a "word of knowledge" way. When this happens, it is one of the clues that God has something for someone with that particular condition. The pain is an indication of a type or location of a physical challenge in someone whom God wants to bless. The challenge is that I do not know who it is for, so I must ask people around me or those who cross my path if it applies to them. I asked the woman who sat next to me if she was having any issues with her left arm, and she was not. In the Uber waiting area, I asked a second lady; she was not having issues with her left arm, but she accepted prayer for her mom with Alzheimer's, even though she was Jewish. I asked my Uber driver if he had any pain or issues with his left arm. The man shared that his left arm had gone totally numb this week while playing golf. I was so thankful in that moment for the accurate word of knowledge that I had received! The driver accepted my offer for prayer and was totally blessed by the encounter. God used this experience to share His love with that driver, and the encounter served as a great encouragement to me to continue taking risks for God to share His love with others.

To truly capture the totality of the ways God expresses His love toward us is impossible to do. As we follow Him and observe what He does in our lives and the lives of others, our appreciation and recognition of His love will grow throughout our lives. We need to love others because He has commanded us to do so, and He set the example by first loving us even when we were enemies to Him. Our motive must always be to love God and love the people He loves so much. When our heart and actions reflect the love of the Father, we will see the miraculous, and God will change our world and shape eternity through our simple obedience and availability.

Conclusion

OBEYING GOD'S command to fulfill the Great Commission is the greatest adventure we could ever ask for. Out of this obedience will flow remarkable fruitfulness in our lives and in the lives of others. As we walk it out, we will have a firsthand account of how God is just as active today in our lives as He was during the ministry of Jesus and the apostles. We will see the ministry of Jesus transforming our lives, our families, our communities, and the places we go. We will see His Kingdom come and His will being done on earth as it is in heaven.

It has been nearly seven years since God called me into a greater availability for Him, and what I have seen Him do has been truly remarkable. The city in which I live is no longer just where I call home. As I travel these streets, the city tells me a story of the faithfulness of God as I remember the beautiful works of God that have taken place on the street corners, in the parks, on the sidewalks, and in parking lots, laundromats, gyms, and so many other places. I recall the faces of the people I have seen healed, set free, and receive Jesus. Just this morning, I was walking my dog with my wife, and I said hello to a neighbor with whom I once prayed and whom God had healed from prostate cancer. I have seen God change this place, and what brings me great joy is that the best is yet to come!

The final thought I want to leave with you is this: *You* are exceptional. You were created from the foundations of the earth with a calling and a purpose. God is the ultimate Artist, and He never does second-rate work. He only does exquisite work, and He did just that when He created you. God does not make duplicates—He only makes originals. Never before has there been anyone like you, and never again will there be another person exactly like you. He put you here at this place in time, in the location you are at, because there is a calling on your life. God has prepared beautiful works for you to walk in. God has given you gifts, talents, equipping, and boldness to carry out what He has planned—works that will change people's lives, alter their eternity, and bring glory to God. God has given you so much, so steward it well for His glory. To whom much is given, much is required. The beautiful thing is that our call is not a drudgery, but it is a precious gift to be lived out and enjoyed. My hope is that our time together has encouraged you. Step out in faith to co-labor with God as He shapes eternity *through your simple availability*. Follow Jesus on the road less traveled. I look forward to hearing about your beautiful exploits and the steadfast faithfulness of God as you make yourself available for Him to work in and through!

For more examples of God's faithfulness or to reach me, visit tolmaoministries.org.

www.ingramcontent.com/pod-product-compliance
Lightning Source LLC
Chambersburg PA
CBHW052220090526
44585CB00015BA/1262